Literature PATTERNS

Written by   Linda Milliken
Design by   Wendy Loreen
Illustrated by   Barb Lorseyedi
Cover illustration by   Mella Cathleen

© 1992 **Edupress** • PO Box 883 • Dana Point, CA 92629

ISBN 1-56472-007-1

2 TABLE OF CONTENTS

SPRING

SUMMER

ABOUT THE BOOK

Literature becomes more than a reading experience when students interact with correlating patterns. Along with the sheer enjoyment of reading aloud, the patterns benefit students by allowing them to develop basic skills.

Recall

• Encourage children to retell the story using patterns to spark their memory.

Sequencing

• Ask, "Which animal (or object) appeared first in the story?" Children select a pattern in response.

Spatial Concepts

• Use patterns to recreate placement of characters in a story.

Creative Thinking

• Develop original stories using the patterns.

Vocabulary Building

• Identify pattern pieces and match them to characters or objects in the stories.

Motor Skill

• Children practice left to write tracking with pattern placement. Some patterns require more intricate manipulation.

HELPS AND HINTS FOR PATTERN CONSTRUCTION

Materials

• Pattern pages are designed to be reproduced on paper, colored and then cut out.
• Patterns may also be traced onto felt and cut out for flannel board use. See additional directions below.

Pattern Requirements

• Each page indicates color for pattern pieces.
• Occasionally there are special NOTES that vary the requirements for felt/flannel board pieces.
• Additional instructions for story integration are also noted in the pattern requirement box.

Permanent Classroom Sets

• Involve parents in coloring, cutting and laminating sets of pattern pieces for small group or individual use.
• Store books and coordinating patterns in zip top bags.

Individual Sets

• Reproduce pages for students to have their own set to color and cut.
• See ADDITIONAL ACTIVITIES on page 6 for more ideas with student sets.

Flannel Board Sets

• Trace patterns onto flannel or felt. Add and glue flannel pieces and trims to create dimension and detail. Use individual pattern illustrations for detail ideas.
• Use for large group or individual interaction.
• See directions on page 7 for making group and individual flannel boards.

HELPS AND HINTS FOR STORY/PATTERN INTEGRATION

Preparation

- Familiarize students with the literature selection's accompanying patterns. This may have already taken place if they created their own individual pattern sets.
- Encourage them to listen closely and be alert for mention of a character, animal or object's pattern.

Integration

- When a character, animal or object with a coordinating pattern makes an appearance in the story, children find the pattern and carry out any action involved.
- Action may include specific placement on or next to patterns already introduced. It may also include interaction between two or more patterns.
- **Large Group**—A flannel board is best suited to serve this purpose. If you do not have a flannel board at your disposal, refer to page 7 for instructions for making inexpensive flannel boards.

  As the story is read, invite students to come to the board, select the pattern that corresponds to an object or character in the story, and place it on the board. Invite other children to respond to the pattern selection, movement and placement.

  Continue reading. When the story is complete, remove the felt pieces and encourage students to retell the story without the use of the book. Children will enjoy the same stories over and over again as they integrate the felt patterns.

- **Individual**—Allow room for students to spread their pattern pieces in front of them. Review the patterns. As characters and objects enter the story, encourage students to find a correlating pattern and place it directly in front of them. Show them how pieces can interact with each other to match the story line.
- **Individual Flannel Boards**—Even if the child is not a reader, he or she can thumb through the book, find coordinating patterns and place them on the mini-flannel board background. Invite volunteers to visit and share a mini-flannel board with a child. The volunteer reads, the student finds the integrating pattern.
- **Small Group**—Gather 4-5 children in a group and work with one set of laminated paper patterns. Take turns selecting patterns. Encourage discussion.

GATHERING THE LITERATURE TITLES

- Reproduce a copy of the table of contents to send home with students. Encourage parents to shop for books on the list to give to the class.
- All books selected are available through libraries and bookstores.

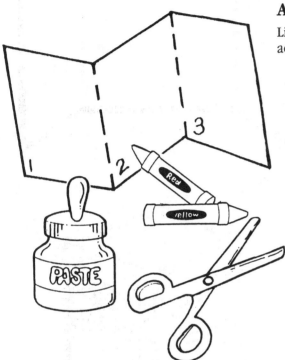

ADDITIONAL ACTIVITIES

Literature patterns lend themselves to a variety of other activities.

- Create individual art. Provide each student with paint or crayons, construction paper and a set of patterns. Ask them to create a background. They can choose to recreate a scene from the book or an original scene. Color, cut and glue patterns to the background. Head a bulletin board with the literature title. Display pictures.
- "Publish" student-made accordion books that retell the story.
- Use as sparks for original creative writing.
- Write rebus stories that use the patterns for words. Retell the story or write an original one.
- Utilize an opaque projector to increase patterns to a size suitable for use as covers for student-written Big Books.
- Use an opaque projector to increase pattern size. Trace the enlarged patterns on a butcher board mural. Invite children to paint the mural.

HELPS AND HINTS FOR FLANNEL BOARD CONSTRUCTION

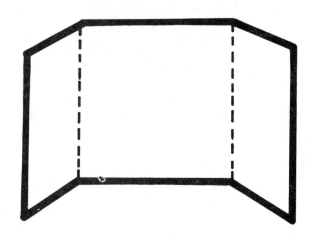

FLANNEL BOARD

Start with a large cardboard box. Cut off the ends and the top. Cut flannel or felt to fit the panels on each side. Spread glue on the panels and apply the material.

FLANNEL BOX

Start with a cardboard box that measures at least 20 inches (50 cm) along each edge. Decide on four permanent backgrounds such as an indoor scene, a country scene, a city scene and an ocean scene. Cover each side of the box with a solid felt background. Paste on the pieces to complete each scene. (You may simply cover each side with felt and eliminate the scenery.)

MINI-FLANNEL BOARD

Cover a shoe box, pencil box, cigar box or gift box with contact paper. Cut a piece of felt to cover the inside lid. Glue in place. Individual books and pattern pieces may be stored inside for student use. They may want to check out the mini-flannel boards to share at home.

MUSICAL MAX

by Robert Kraus
Simon & Schuster Inc.

STORY SUMMARY

A hippo develops his musical talent on a variety of instruments, much to his neighbors' distress—until he stops practicing.

Helps & Hints for story integration and pattern construction found on pages 4-5.

Related Learning:
- Listening
- Sound discrimination
- Feelings—moods
- Values—consideration

More To Do:
- Listen to and learn to identify a variety of musical instruments.
- Form your own classroom band.

harmonica

Pattern Requirements:
- One blue harmonica
- One yellow triangle
- One brown violin

triangle

trombone

bass

Pattern Requirements:
- One yellow trombone
- One brown bass

MUSICAL MAX

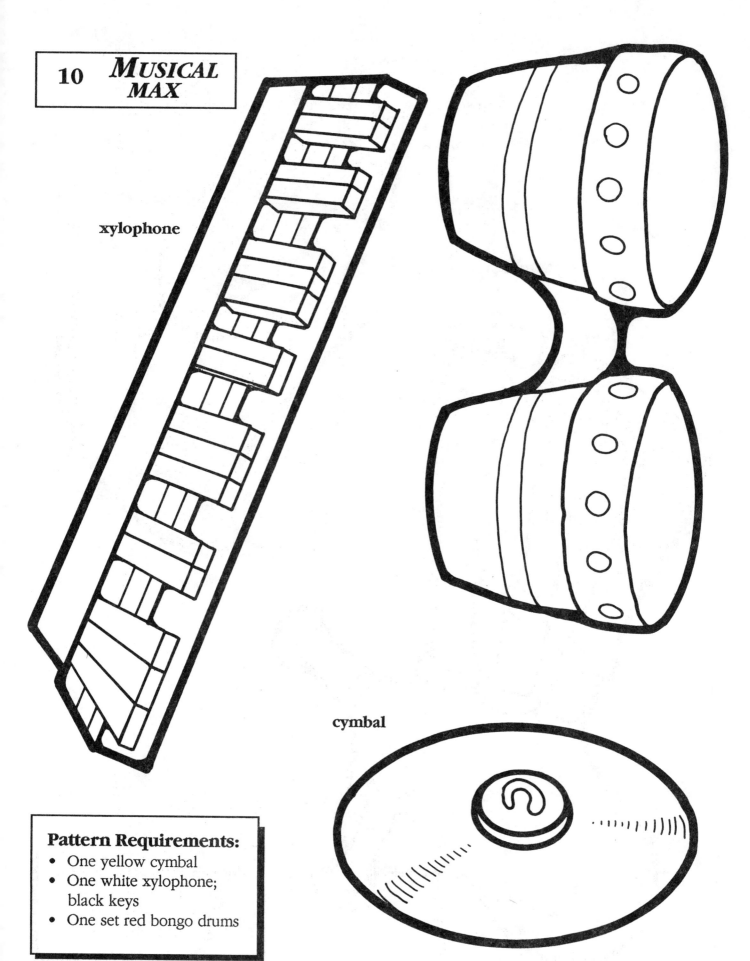

xylophone

cymbal

Pattern Requirements:
- One yellow cymbal
- One white xylophone; black keys
- One set red bongo drums

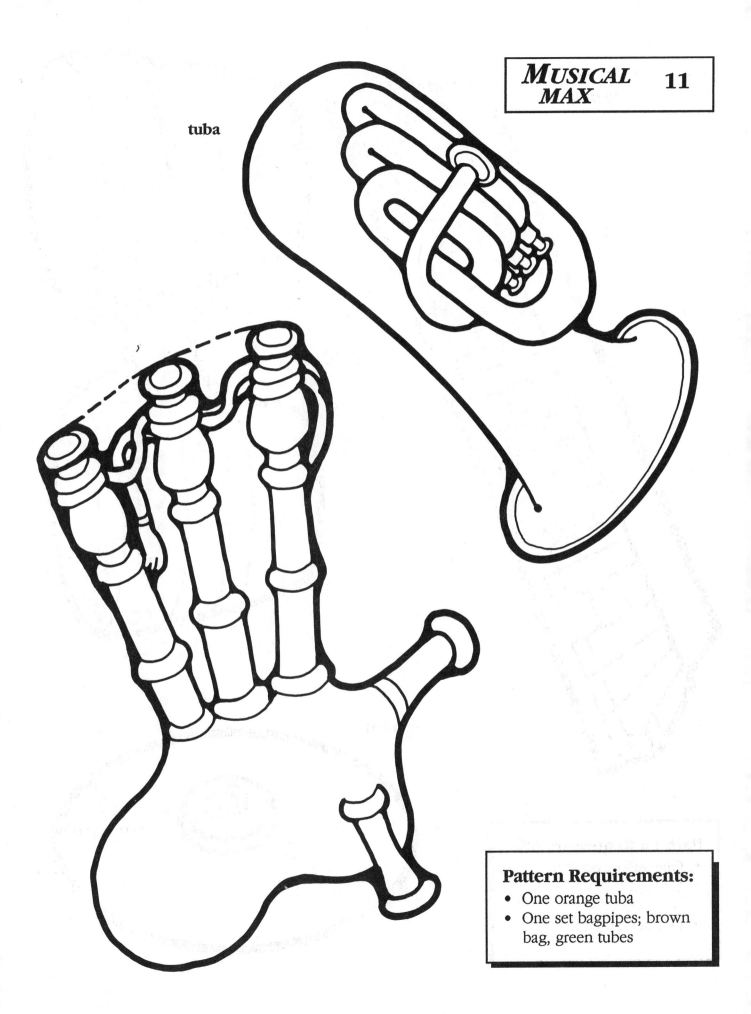

tuba

Pattern Requirements:
- One orange tuba
- One set bagpipes; brown bag, green tubes

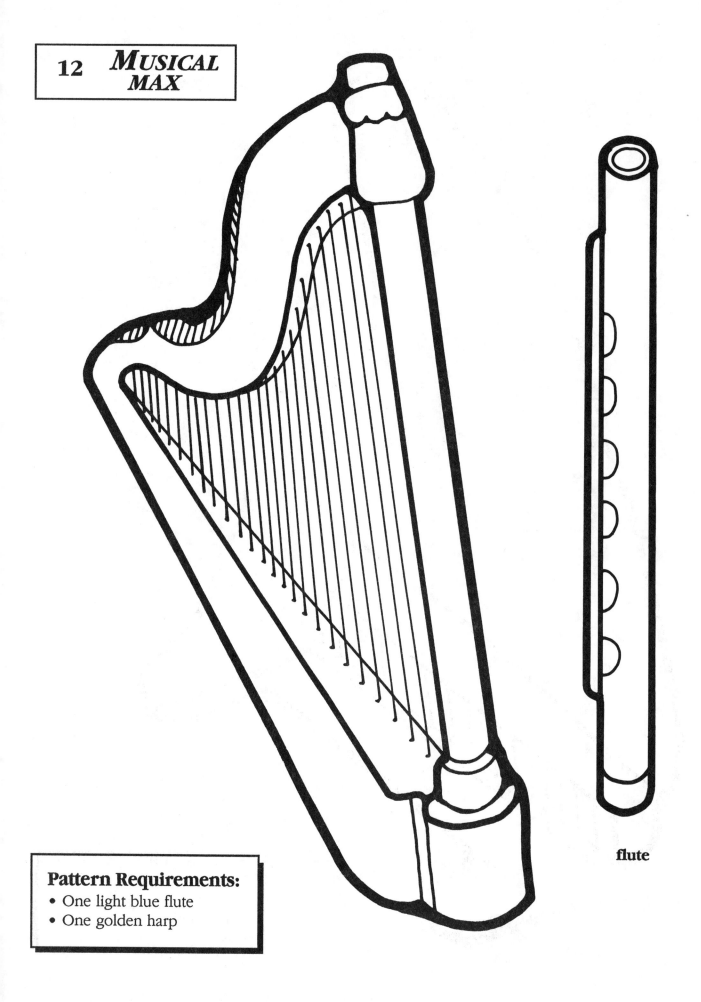

flute

Pattern Requirements:
- One light blue flute
- One golden harp

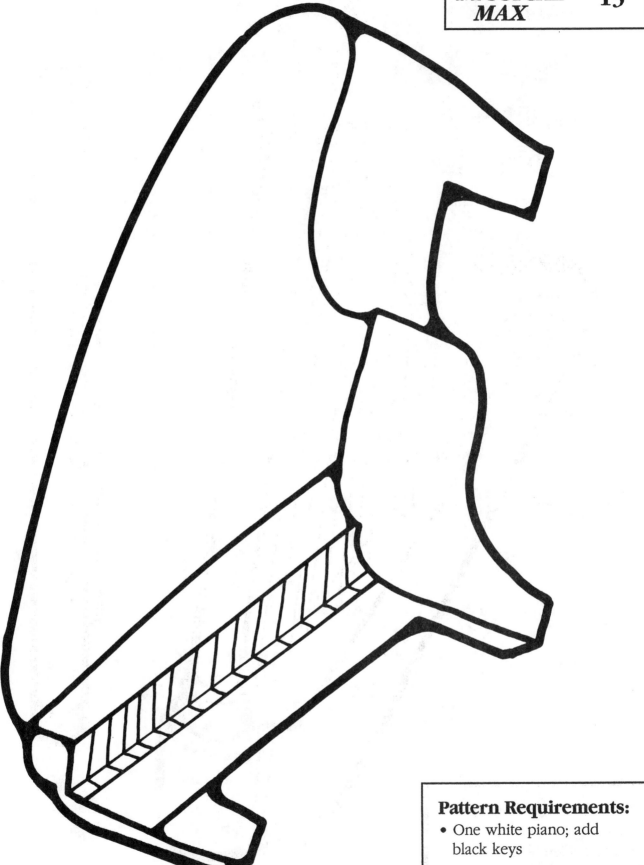

Pattern Requirements:
- One white piano; add black keys

GOODNIGHT MOON

by Margaret Wise Brown
Harper LB

STORY SUMMARY

It's bedtime. Help a bunny say goodnight, one by one, to all the familiar things in its room.

Helps & Hints for story integration and pattern construction found on pages 4-5.

Related Learning:
- Oral language
- Recall
- Sharing—bring a stuffed animal
- Rhyming

More To Do:
- Paint a picture of a nighttime moon.
- Talk about some of the things you do at bedtime.

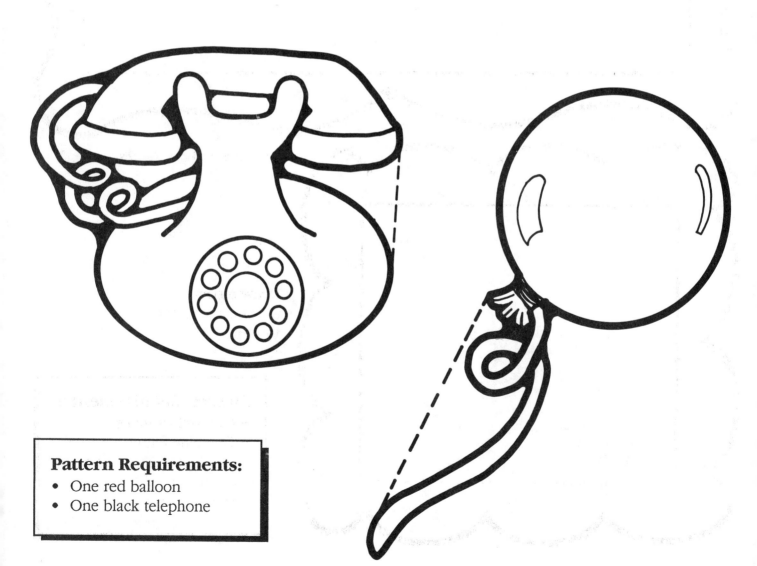

Pattern Requirements:
- One red balloon
- One black telephone

Draw three bears

Draw a cow
jumping over the
moon.

Pattern Requirements:
- One yellow frame
- One blue frame
  Draw pictures or paste
  cut-outs in each frame as
  indicated

Pattern Requirements:
- One white kitten
- One gray kitten
- Red mittens
- One white mouse

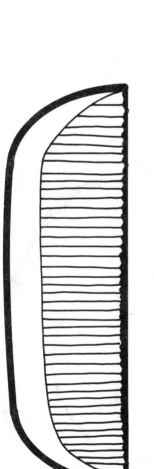

Pattern Requirements:
- One yellow comb
- One yellow brush
- One red toy house

Pattern Requirements:
- One yellow moon
- One blue light with a yellow shade
- One red bowl filled with white mush

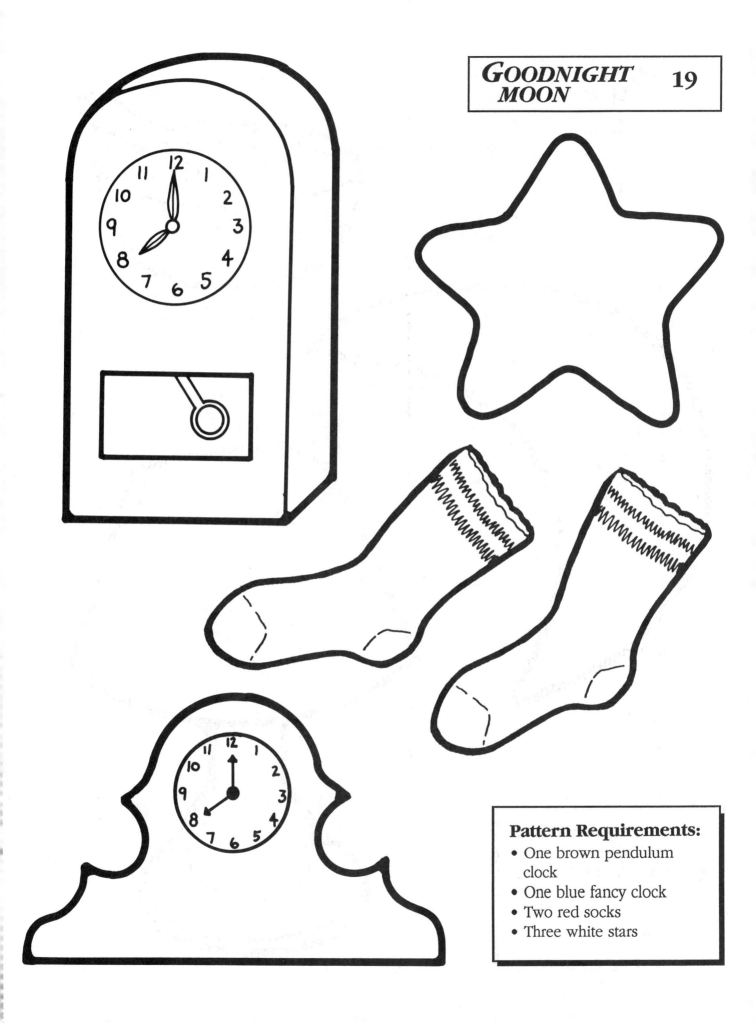

Pattern Requirements:
- One brown pendulum clock
- One blue fancy clock
- Two red socks
- Three white stars

STORY SUMMARY

Repetitive verse lends appeal to this story of a nighttime adventure shared by two skeletons.

THE BLACK CAT

by Allan Ahlberg
Greenwillow Books

Helps & Hints for story integration and pattern construction found on pages 4-5.

Related Learning:
- Size comparison
- Repetition
- Sorting
- Camouflage

More To Do:
- Make a bone pile of small, medium and large bones; sort by size
- Memorize the repeated verse; make up new sled occupants

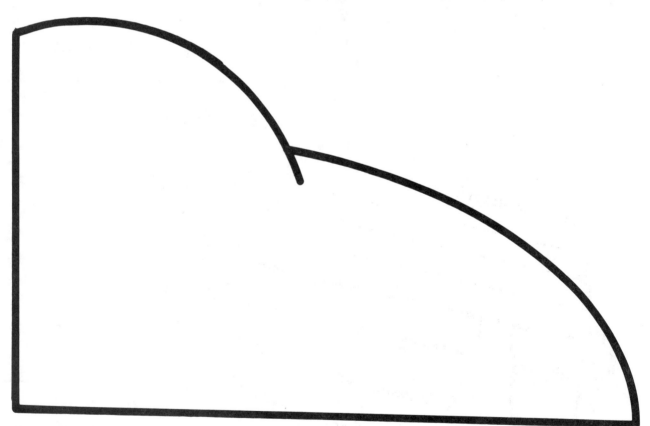

Pattern Requirements:
- One black slope
- One white slope

Pattern Requirements:
- One red sled
- Four yellow stars
- One black cat

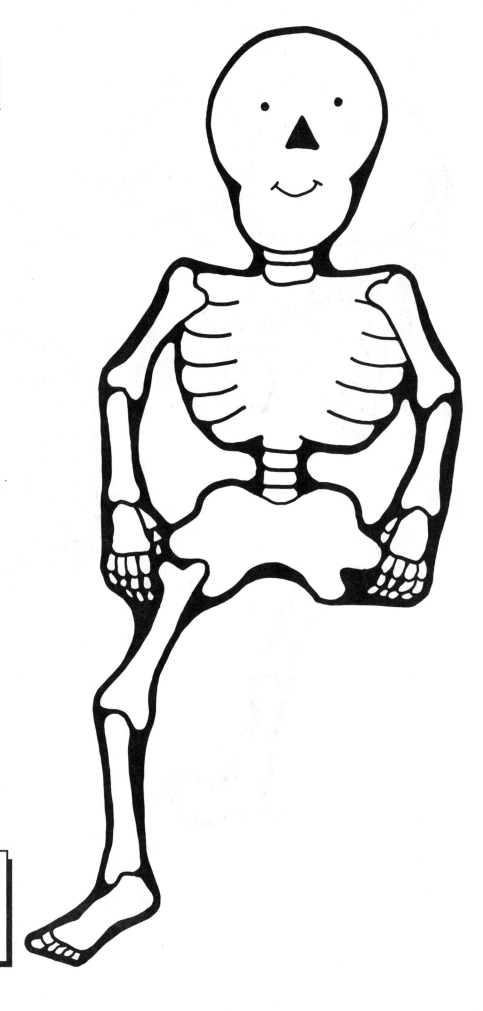

Pattern Requirements:
- One large white skeleton torso
- Four white skeleton legs

Pattern Requirements:
- One white skeleton torso
- Four white skeleton legs
- One white skeleton dog

BIG PUMPKIN

by Erica Silverman
Macmillan Publishing Co.

Helps & Hints for story integration and pattern construction found on pages 4-5.

Related Learning:
- Size Comparison
- Values—cooperation
- Order

More To Do:
- Bake a pumpkin pie or other pumpkin treat to enjoy together.
- Plant some pumpkin seeds and watch for growth.

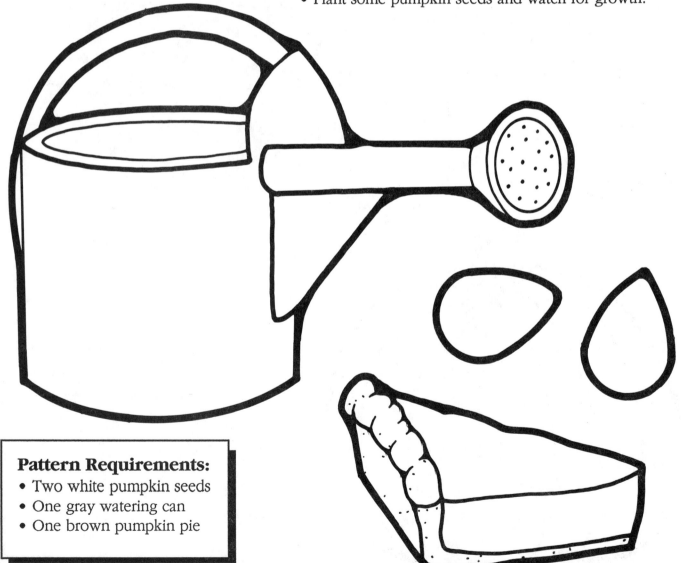

Pattern Requirements:
- Two white pumpkin seeds
- One gray watering can
- One brown pumpkin pie

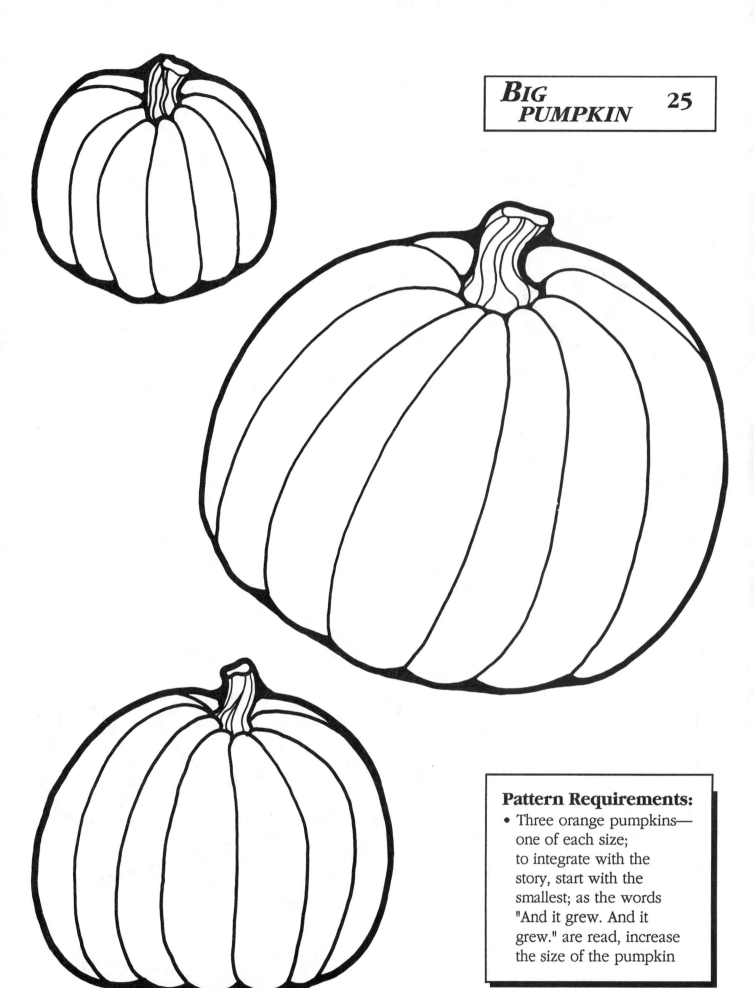

Pattern Requirements:
• Three orange pumpkins—
one of each size;
to integrate with the
story, start with the
smallest; as the words
"And it grew. And it
grew." are read, increase
the size of the pumpkin

Pattern Requirements:
- One white ghost
- One black bat
- One green witch with orange hair black hat and dress

Pattern Requirements:
- One white mummy
- One gray vampire with a black and red cape

HIDE AND SNAKE

by Keith Baker
Harcourt, Brace, Jovanovich

STORY SUMMARY

A brightly colored snake challenges readers to a game of hide-and-seek as he hides among familiar objects.

Helps & Hints for story integration and pattern construction found on pages 4-5.

Related Learning:
- Visual discrimination
- Vocabulary development
- Small motor skills

More To Do:
- Use ribbon—wrap, loop, curl, weave and twist—to develop small motor skills
- Learn to weave a simple pattern; make a wall hanging

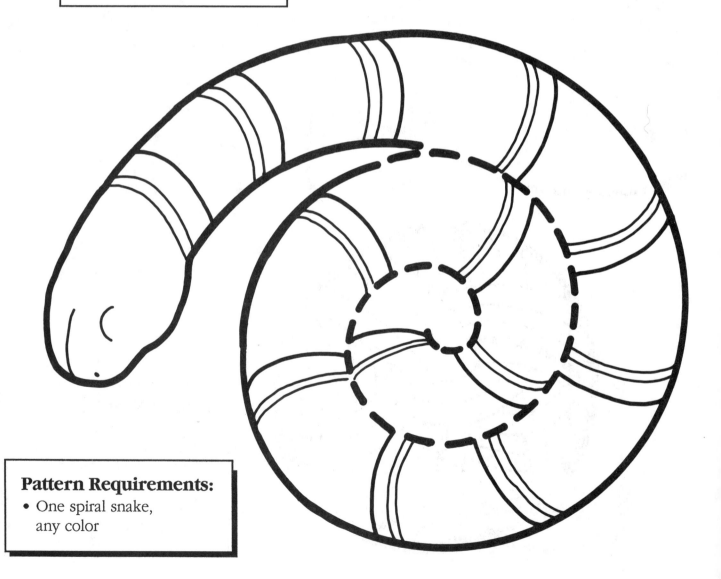

Pattern Requirements:
- One spiral snake, any color

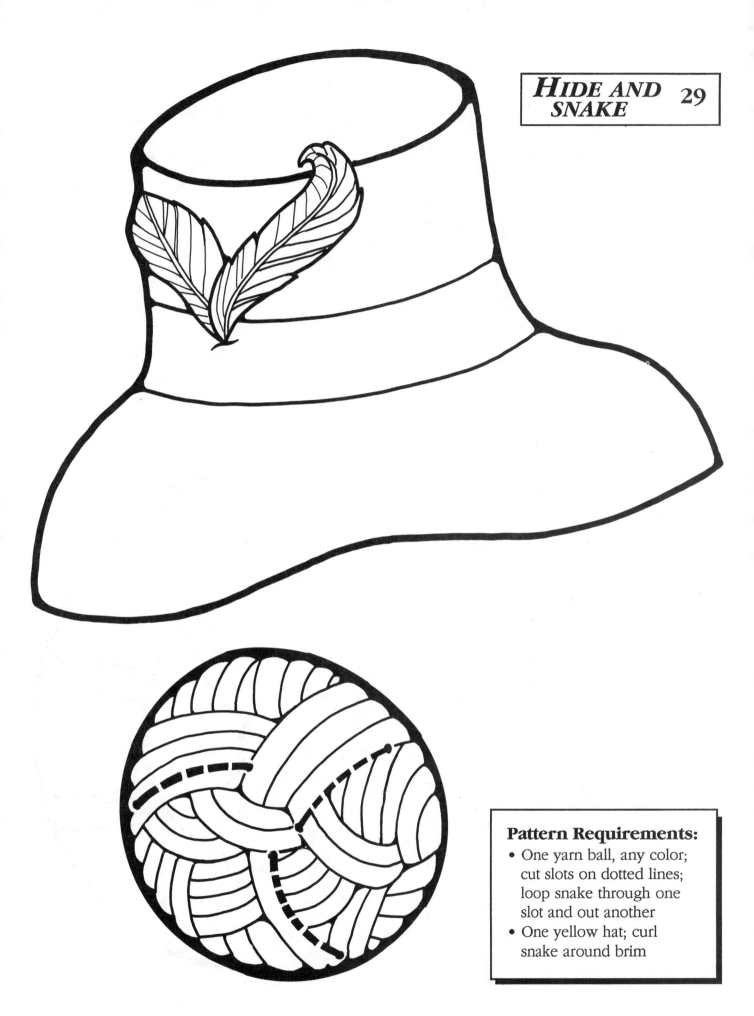

Pattern Requirements:
- One yarn ball, any color; cut slots on dotted lines; loop snake through one slot and out another
- One yellow hat; curl snake around brim

Pattern Requirements:

- One blue present; color or cut a different color bow; wrap snake around the present
- One red sock; cut slots on dotted lines; slide snake through the slots
- One purple vase; cut slots on doted lines; twist snake around the vase and through the slots

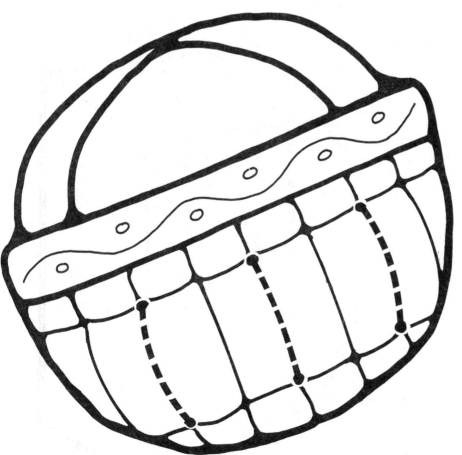

Pattern Requirements:
- One basket; cut slots on dotted line; weave snake in and out through the slots
- One white shoe; punch a hole in each circle; thread with a shoelace; tangle snake in lace

STORY SUMMARY

A wolf and a mother hen try to trick each other—all over a pot of soup made from a stone.

STONE SOUP

by Tony Ross
Dial Books for Young Readers

Helps & Hints for story integration and pattern construction found on pages 4-5.

Related Learning:
- Sequencing
- Nutrition
- Oral language
- Values—sharing

More To Do:
- Identify and sample a variety of vegetables.
- Make a shared soup—one in which everyone contributes an ingredient.

stone

Pattern Requirements:
- One gray spoon
- One brown stone
- One each; white salt and pepper shakers; spread with glue and sprinkle with actual spices (optional)

Pattern Requirements:
• One white pot

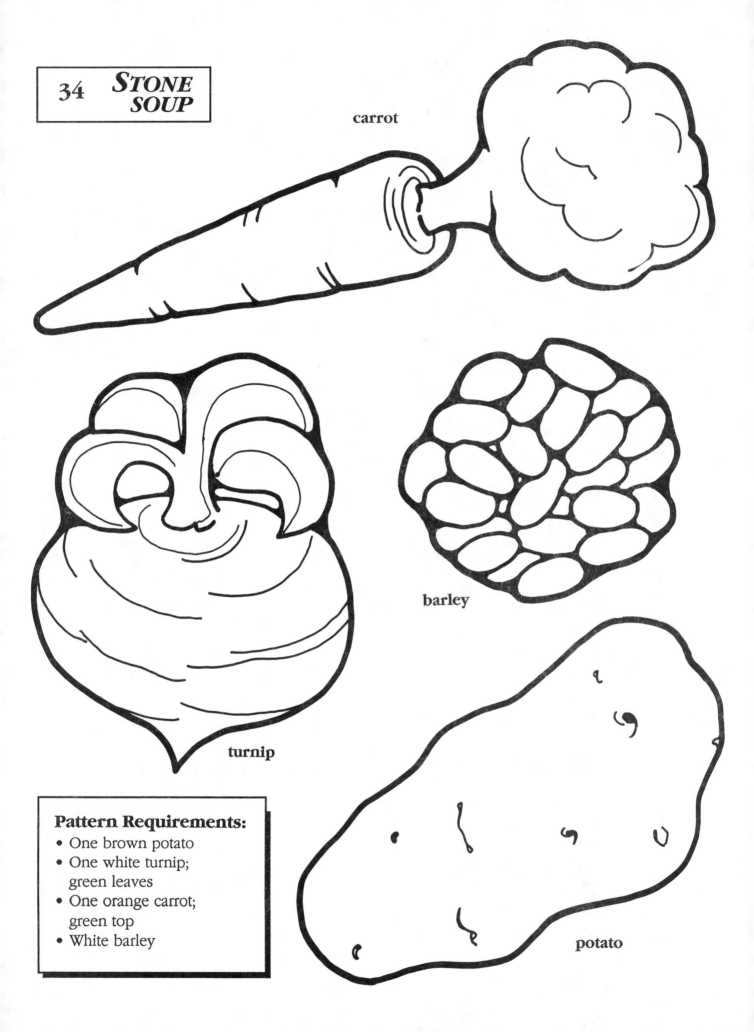

carrot

barley

turnip

potato

Pattern Requirements:
- One brown potato
- One white turnip; green leaves
- One orange carrot; green top
- White barley

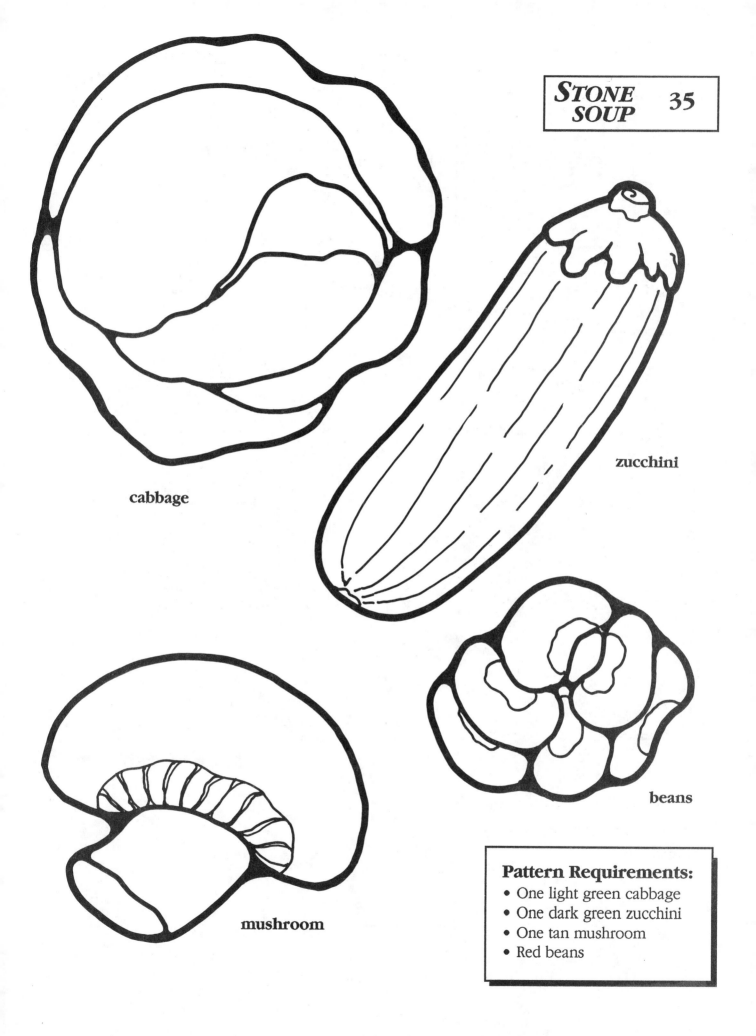

cabbage

zucchini

mushroom

beans

Pattern Requirements:
- One light green cabbage
- One dark green zucchini
- One tan mushroom
- Red beans

STORY SUMMARY

Several animals sleep snugly in Nicki's lost mitten until the bear sneezes—A Ukrainian folktale.

THE MITTEN

by Jan Brett
G.P. Putnam's Sons

Helps & Hints for story integration and pattern construction found on pages 4-5.

Related Learning:
- Legends and folktales
- Values; getting along with others

More To Do:
- Hang personalized mittens (real or paper) from a clothesline; tuck notes and rewards inside
- Experiment with a variety of materials to test stretching capabilities

mole

hedgehog

Pattern Requirements:
- One grey mole
- One white rabbit
- One tan hedgehog

Pattern Requirements:
• Two white mittens—
staple, glue or stitch
around all sides, leaving
bottom open so animals
can be tucked inside as
the story progresses

badger

Pattern Requirements:
- One brown owl
- One black badger—add white stripes
- One golden fox

Pattern Requirements:
- One brown bear
- One tan mouse

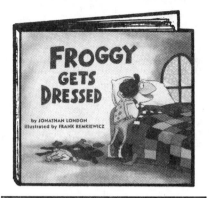

STORY SUMMARY

Froggy complicates his efforts to get himself dressed for a day of play in the snow.

FROGGY GETS DRESSED

by Jonathan London
Viking

Helps & Hints for story integration and pattern construction found on pages 4-5.

Related Learning:
- Sequential order
- Making choices
- Small motor
- Values—consideration

More To Do:
- Practice buttoning, tying, matching and other "getting dressed" skills.
- Have a relay race that involves putting on and taking off layers of clothing.

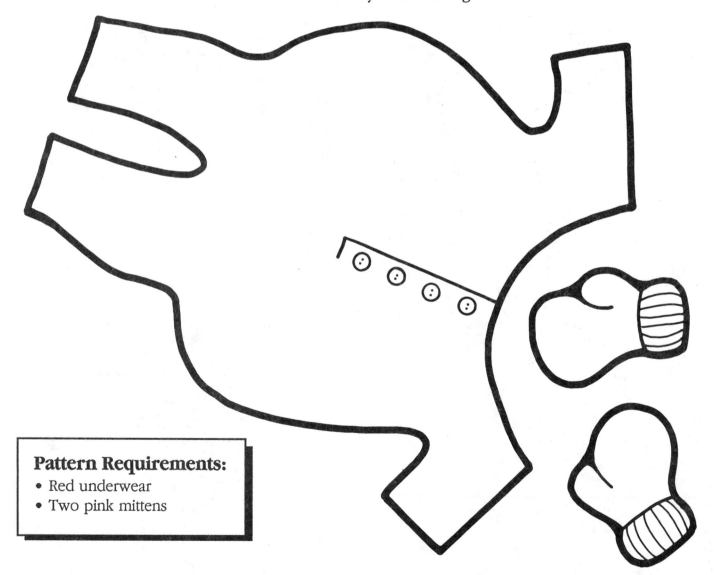

Pattern Requirements:
- Red underwear
- Two pink mittens

Pattern Requirements:
• One light green frog

FROGGY GETS DRESSED

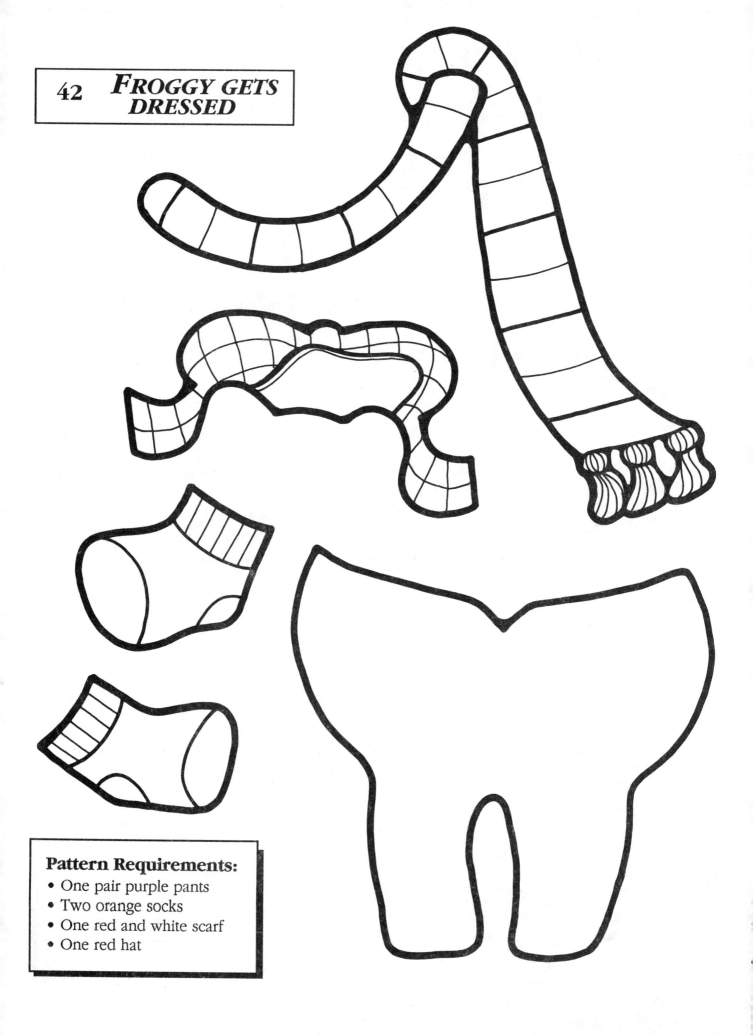

Pattern Requirements:
- One pair purple pants
- Two orange socks
- One red and white scarf
- One red hat

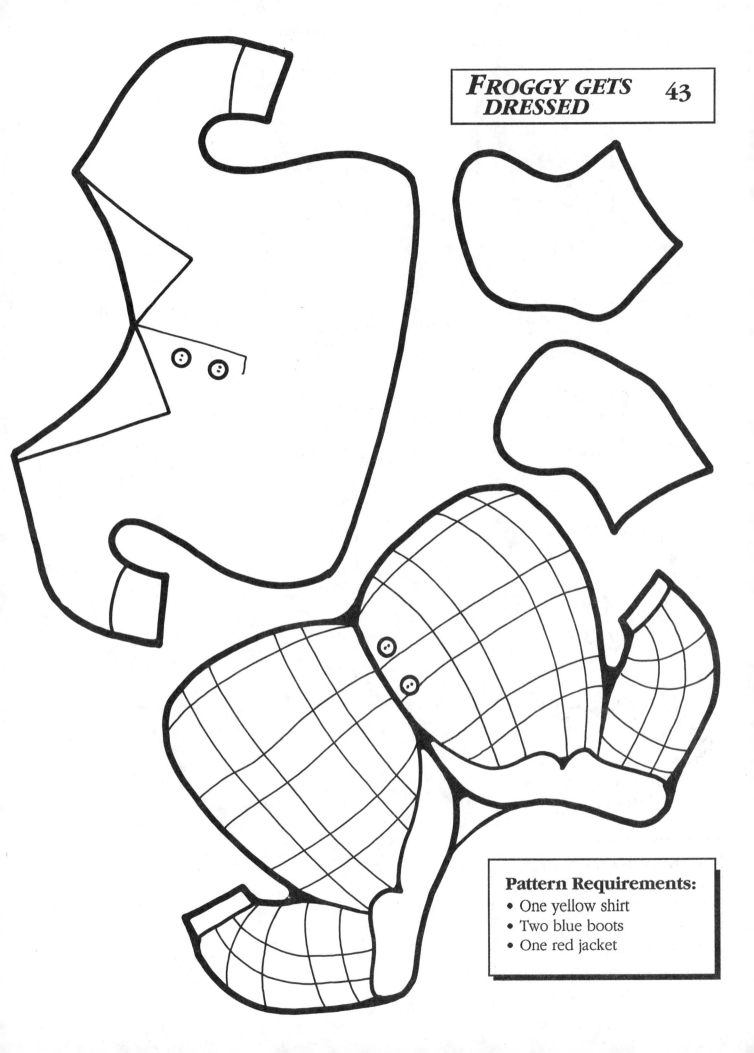

Pattern Requirements:
- One yellow shirt
- Two blue boots
- One red jacket

IMOGENE'S ANTLERS by David Small
Crown

Helps & Hints for story integration and pattern construction found on pages 4-5.

STORY SUMMARY

When Imogene wakes up with antlers, she faces some problems carrying out her everyday routines.

Related Learning:
- Problem solving
- Motor development
- Feelings—being different from others

More To Do:
- Practice hanging things on hooks and hangers.
- Make paper antlers to wear on your head for the day.

Pattern Requirements:
- One yellow chandelier; Hook the antlers on the chandelier

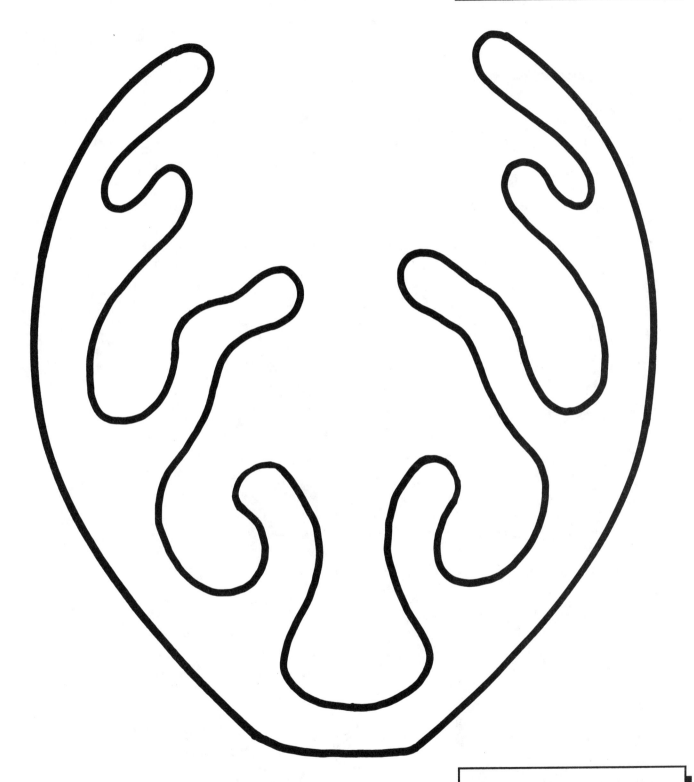

Pattern Requirements:
• Brown antlers

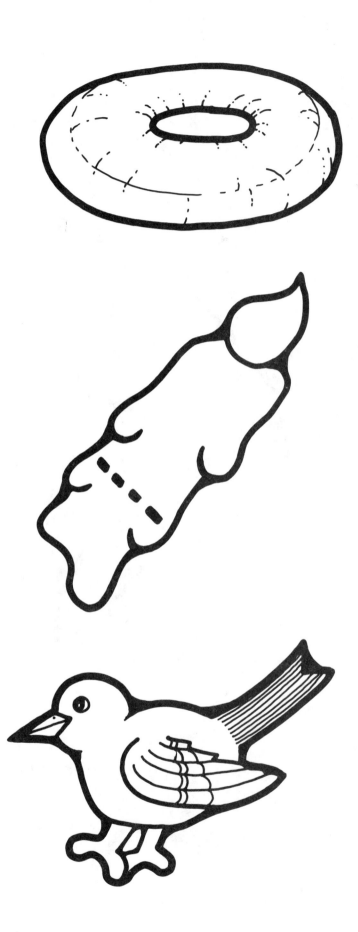

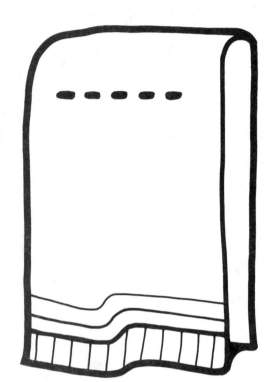

Pattern Requirements:

- One yellow towel; cut on dotted line; hook on antlers
- One brown doughnut; cut out hole in center; hook on antlers
- One red bird; perch on top of antlers
- One white candle; yellow flame; cut on dotted lines; hook on antlers

NOTE: If cutting felt shapes for flannel board use, make several of each in different colors.

Pattern Requirements:
• One hat; glue ribbon and trim to personalize; fit over antlers

SANTA MOUSE
by Michael Brown
Grosset & Dunlap

STORY SUMMARY

A thoughtful mouse leaves a gift for Santa and becomes his special helper—complete with miniature Santa suit.

Helps & Hints for story integration and pattern construction found on pages 4-5.

Related Learning:
- Rhyming words
- Values—traditions
- Roleplaying

More To Do:
- Make a paper beard and pretend to be Santa Claus.
- Make a special gift to leave for Santa Claus.

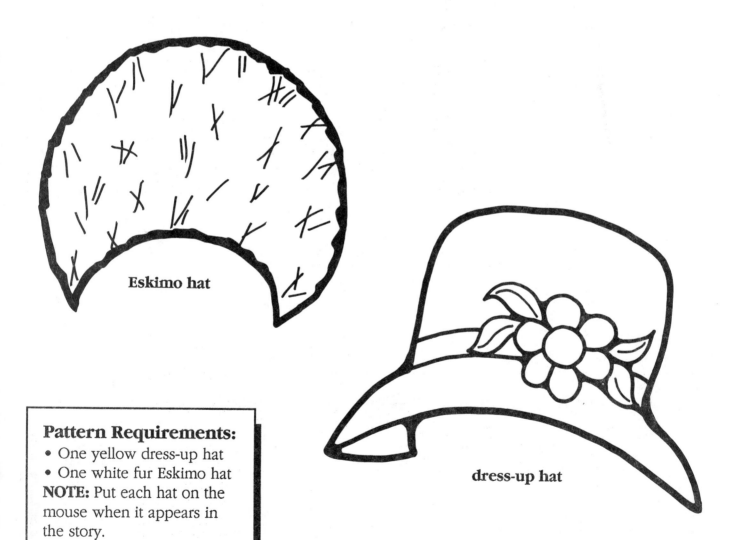

Eskimo hat

dress-up hat

Pattern Requirements:
- One yellow dress-up hat
- One white fur Eskimo hat
NOTE: Put each hat on the mouse when it appears in the story.

Spanish hat

cowboy hat

Pattern Requirements:
- One light brown mouse
- One dark brown cowboy hat
- One black Spanish hat

Pattern Requirements:
- Two black boots
- One red Santa suit; black belt, white cottonball trim (optional)
- One red Santa hat; white cottonball trim (optional)
- One white beard

Pattern Requirements:
- One red sleigh
- One Santa Claus; color suit and trims accordingly; optional cotton ball trim for beard

STORY SUMMARY

Repetitive verse features zoo animals and the unusual sounds they make.

POLAR BEAR, POLAR BEAR

by Bill Martin Jr.
Henry Holt and Co.

Helps & Hints for story integration and pattern construction found on pages 4-5.

Related Learning:
- Animal Identification
- Sound discrimination
- Rhythmic repetition

More To Do:
- Take a field trip to a nearby zoo. Identify the animals.
- Try to make the sounds that animals make.

Pattern Requirements:
- One purple walrus

Pattern Requirements:
- One white polar bear
- One black and white zebra

Pattern Requirements:
- One orange lion
- One green boa constrictor; yellow spots

Pattern Requirements:
- One blue hippopotamus
- One yellow leopard; brown spots

Pattern Requirements:
• One gray elephant

Pattern Requirements:
- One pink flamingo
- One bright blue peacock; rainbow-colored spots

STORY SUMMARY

All members of a household try to take a long winter's nap. A wakeful flea disturbs the plan.

THE NAPPING HOUSE

by Audrey Wood
Harcourt

Helps & Hints for story integration and pattern construction found on pages 4-5.

Related Learning:
- Size relationships
- Memory development
- Repetition
- Vocabulary development

More To Do:
- Choose unrelated objects to put in piles, largest object at the bottom.
- Act out the adjectives accompanying each character—dozing, snoring, thumping, etc.

flea

Pattern Requirements:
- One white dog
- One yellow cat
- One black flea

NOTE: Stack the characters in the bed, bottom to top; then unstack them as the story progresses.

Pattern Requirements:
- One light blue house

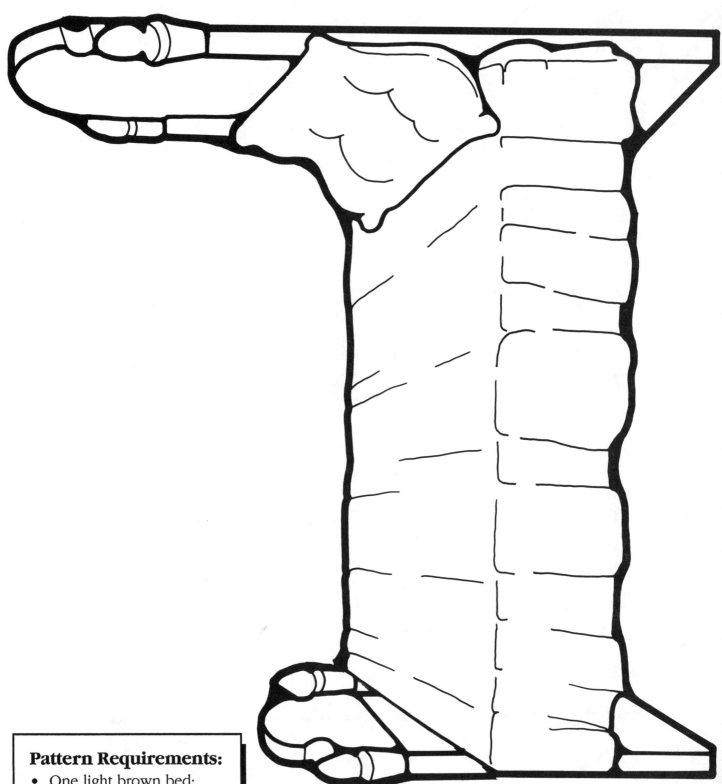

Pattern Requirements:
- One light brown bed;
  light blue bedspread

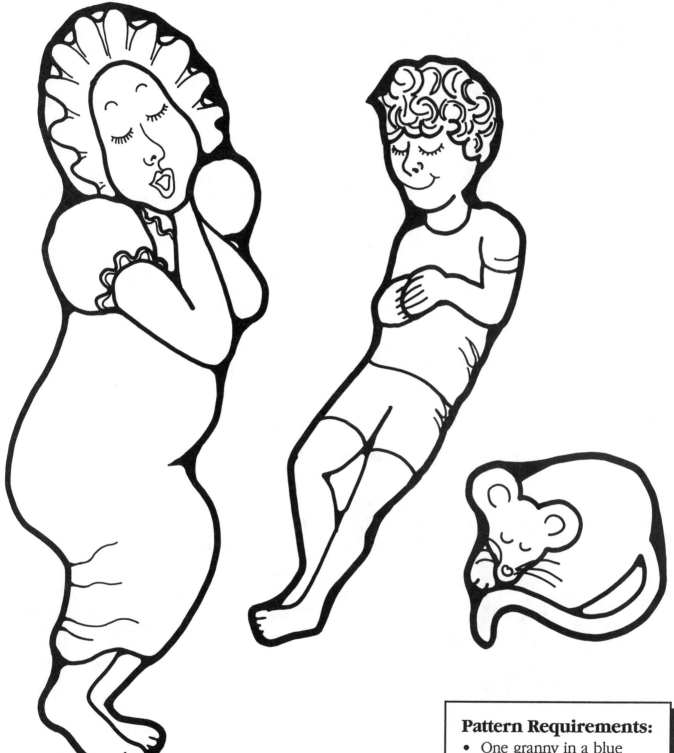

Pattern Requirements:
- One granny in a blue gown.
- One boy in green pajamas

MONKEY SOUP

by Louis Scahar
Alfred A. Knopf

STORY SUMMARY

A girl makes her own unusual version of "get-well" soup for her father.

Helps & Hints for story integration and pattern construction found on pages 4-5.

Related Learning:
- Sequencing
- Oral expression
- Feelings
- Values—caring for family and friends

More To Do:
- Make more imaginary soup. Paint a batch of soup for a sick elephant—or yourself.
- Talk about feelings. What things make children laugh or feel happy?

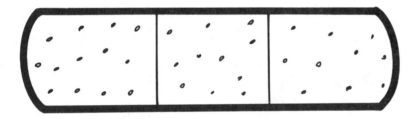

Pattern Requirements:
- One pink bandage
- One blue crayon
- One green toothbrush

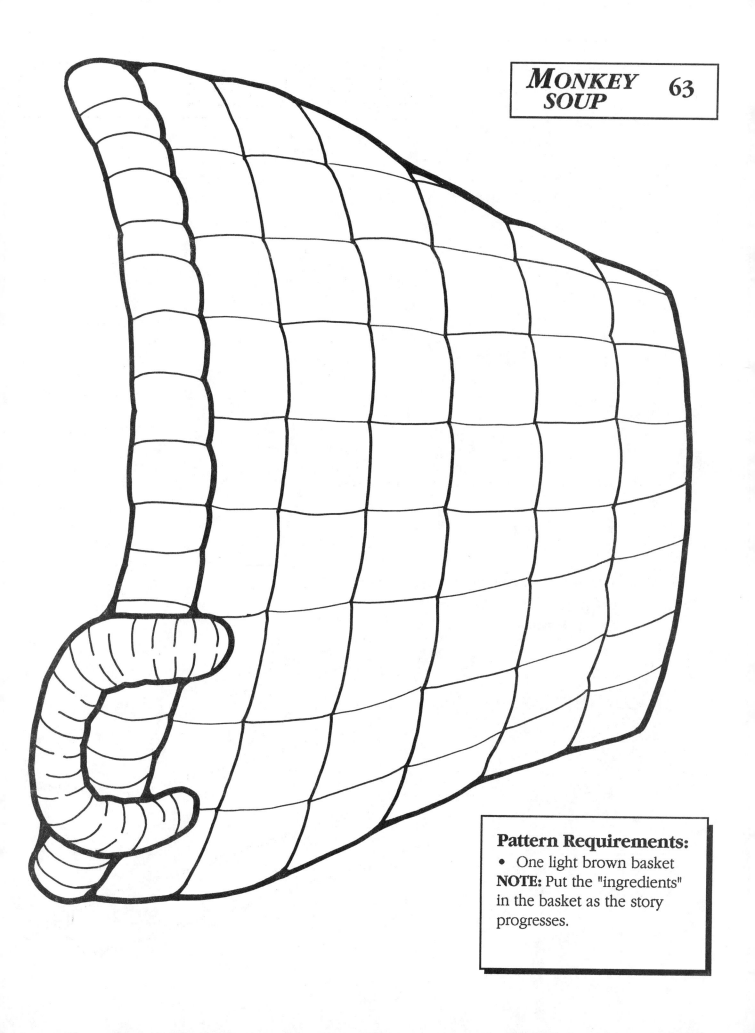

Pattern Requirements:
• One light brown basket
NOTE: Put the "ingredients" in the basket as the story progresses.

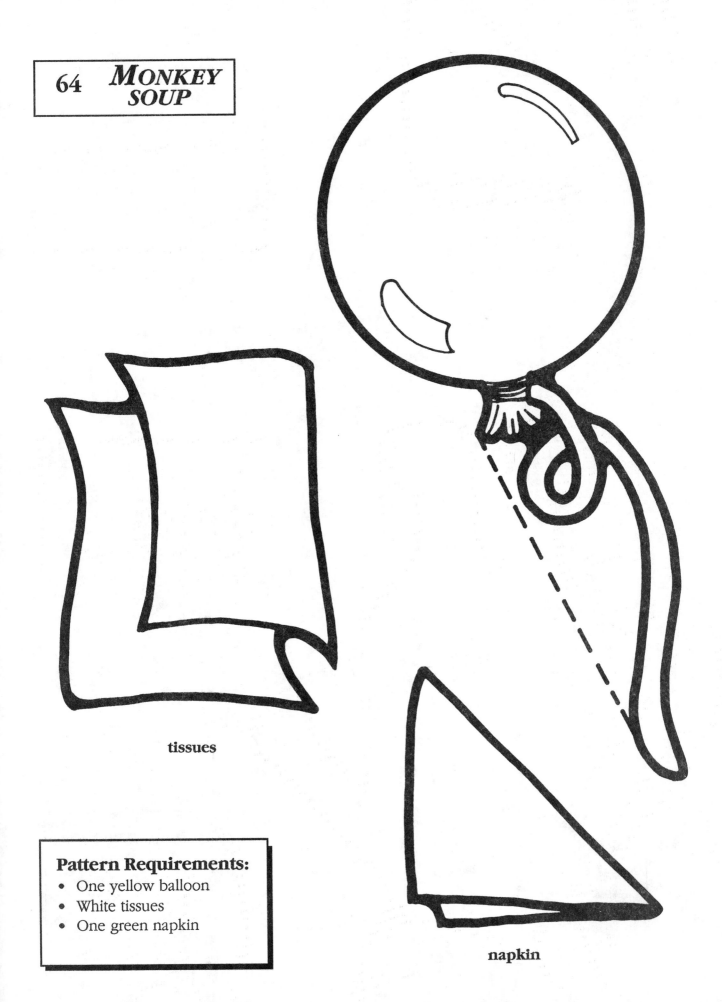

tissues

napkin

Pattern Requirements:
- One yellow balloon
- White tissues
- One green napkin

Pattern Requirements:
- One brown monkey

SOAP

Pattern Requirements:
- One orange bar of soap
- One yellow blanket

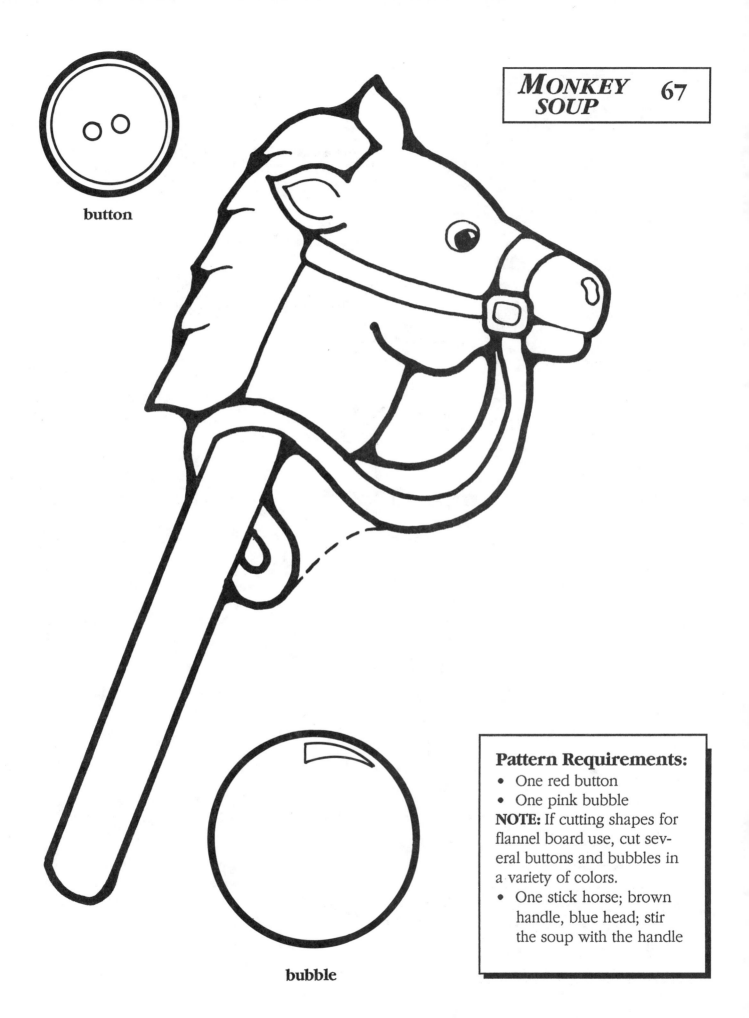

button

bubble

Pattern Requirements:
- One red button
- One pink bubble

NOTE: If cutting shapes for flannel board use, cut several buttons and bubbles in a variety of colors.

- One stick horse; brown handle, blue head; stir the soup with the handle

THE SHEEP FOLLOW

by Monica Wellington
Dutton Children's Books

STORY SUMMARY

While the shepherd slumbers, the sheep romp with other animals through the barnyard—until they wake the shepherd.

Helps & Hints for story integration and pattern construction found on pages 4-5.

Related Learning:
- Ordinal numbers
- Sequencing
- Animals

More To Do:
- Pretend you are animals and play "follow the leader".
- Identify farm animals. Paint a barnyard mural.

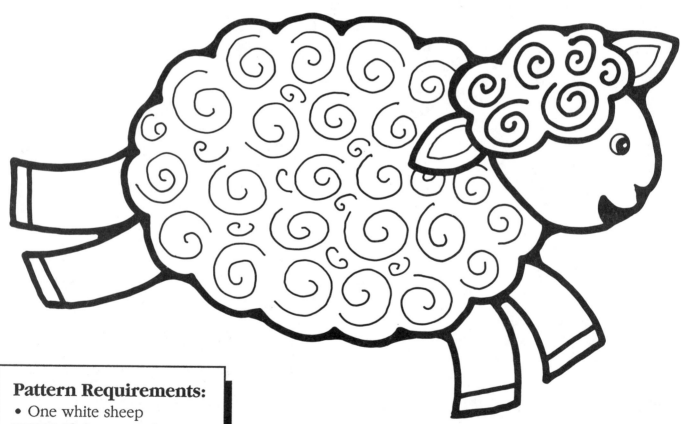

Pattern Requirements:
- One white sheep

NOTE: If shapes are being cut for flannel board use, cut several sheep, some black,

goose

Pattern Requirements:
- One shepherd with blue pants; red and white striped shirt
- One white goose
- One orange fish

Pattern Requirements:
- One red barnyard fence

corn

Pattern Requirements:

- One green stalk of corn
- One white rabbit
- One yellow butterfly

Pattern Requirements:
- One pink pig;
  let the pig munch on the
  stalk of corn
- One black cat;
  walk the cat along the
  barnyard fence

duck

Pattern Requirements:
- One yellow duck

NOTE: If cutting ducks for flannel board use, cut three.
- One white dog; black spots, red collar

PLANTING A RAINBOW

by Lois Ehlert
Voyager Books

STORY SUMMARY

Follow the colorful growth of a garden, from planting the bulbs in the fall to watching the flowers produce a rainbow of blooms.

Helps & Hints for story integration and pattern construction found on pages 4-5.

Related Learning:
- Color recognition
- Progression, sequencing
- Directionality—above and below

More To Do:
- Plant and grow bulbs in individual containers
- Collect seed packets; grow flowers; take a flower walk

soil line

Pattern Requirements:
- One brown soil line
- Seven bulbs:
  - 2-orange
  - 1-blue
  - 1-red
  - 1-yellow
  - 2-purple
- Ten green stems— no pattern

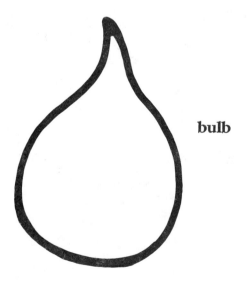

bulb

tiger lily

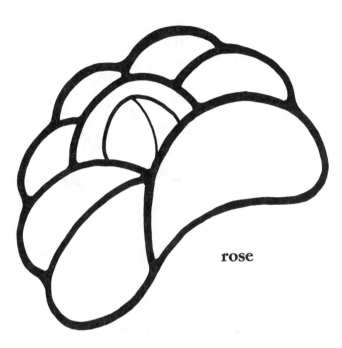

rose

poppy

tulip

Pattern Requirements:
- One red tulip
- One red rose
- One orange poppy
- One orange tiger lily

daisy

daffodil

fern

leaf

Pattern Requirements:
- One yellow daisy
- One yellow daffodil
- One green fern
- Five green leaves

cornflower

morning glory

violet

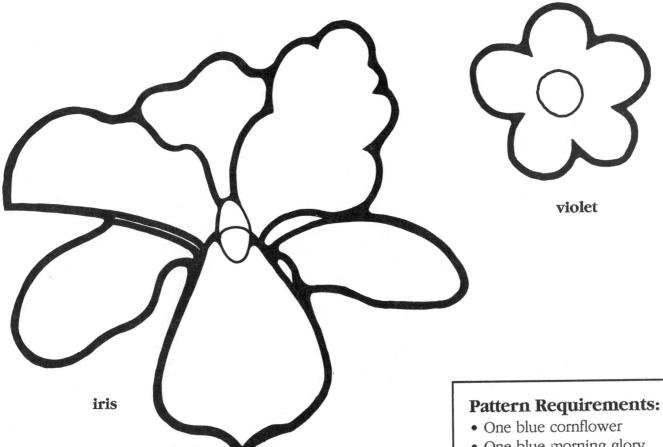

iris

Pattern Requirements:
- One blue cornflower
- One blue morning glory
- One purple violet
- One purple iris

SEVEN EGGS

by Meredith Hooper
HarperCollins

STORY SUMMARY

Seven eggs hatch a different animal each day of the week—with a surprise on the last day!

Helps & Hints for story integration and pattern construction found on pages 4-5.

Related Learning:
- Days of the week
- Counting

More To Do:
- Role play an animal seeing the world for the first time
- Find out about the differences between animal eggs

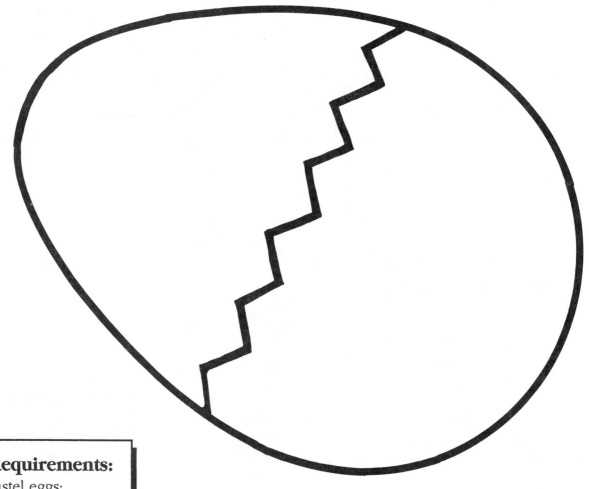

Pattern Requirements:
- Seven pastel eggs; cut across zigzag lines

Pattern Requirements:
- One black penguin; add a white oval tummy and yellow triangular beak
- One green crocodile

Pattern Requirements:
- One light brown ostrich
- One dark brown lizard

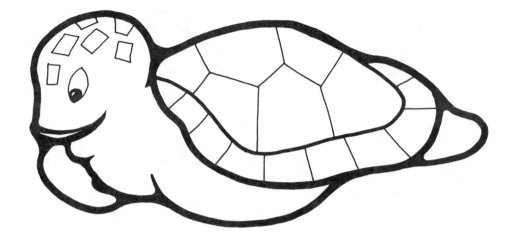

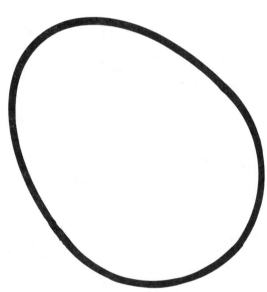

Pattern Requirements:
- One green turtle
- One white barn owl
- Seven brown eggs

STORY SUMMARY

A little bunny sets off to spend a day on its own for the first time.

WHAT DO BUNNIES DO ALL DAY?

by Judy Mastrangelo
Ideals Children's Books

Helps & Hints for story integration and pattern construction found on pages 4-5.

Related Learning:

- Recall
- Memory development
- Values—Independence
- Same and different

More To Do:

- Make a list of things the bunny did. Ask children to recall and list *their* daily activities. Are any similar?
- Invite parents to visit and describe their daily schedule.

Pattern Requirements:

- One light brown bunny

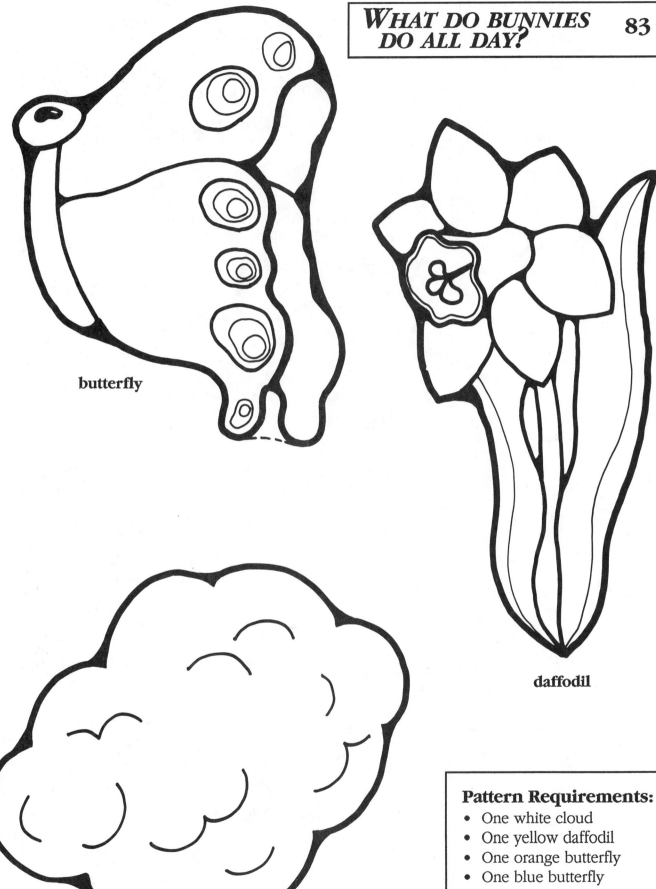

butterfly

daffodil

Pattern Requirements:
- One white cloud
- One yellow daffodil
- One orange butterfly
- One blue butterfly

raspberries

small bush

bee

Pattern Requirements:

- One bunch red raspberries
- One green bush; let bunny sleep under the bush
- One black bee

stream

Pattern Requirements:
- One yellow sun
- One blue stream

OVER THE MEADOW

by Ezra Jack Keats
Scholastic, Inc.

STORY SUMMARY

A simple counting book introduces animals and insects—and their offspring—in their natural habitats.

Helps & Hints for story integration and pattern construction found on pages 4-5.

Related Learning:
- animal habitat
- counting
- pantomime
- rhyming

More To Do:
- Pantomime the actions of all the animal and insects found in the story.
- Take a nature walk; make a mural of animal homes.

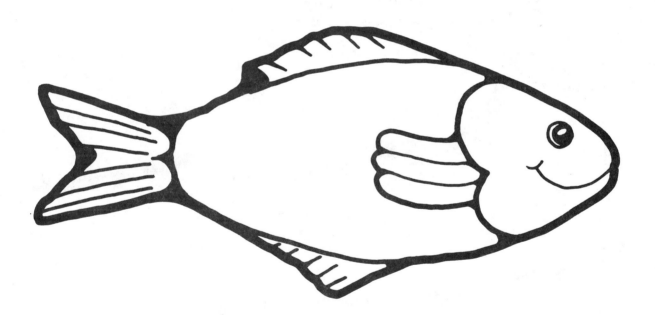

Pattern Requirements:
- One large green fish
- One small green fish

NOTE: If cutting shapes for flannel board use or for counting, cut two small green fish.

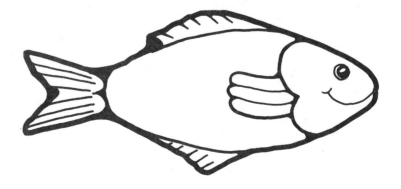

Pattern Requirements:
- One large brown turtle
- One small brown turtle

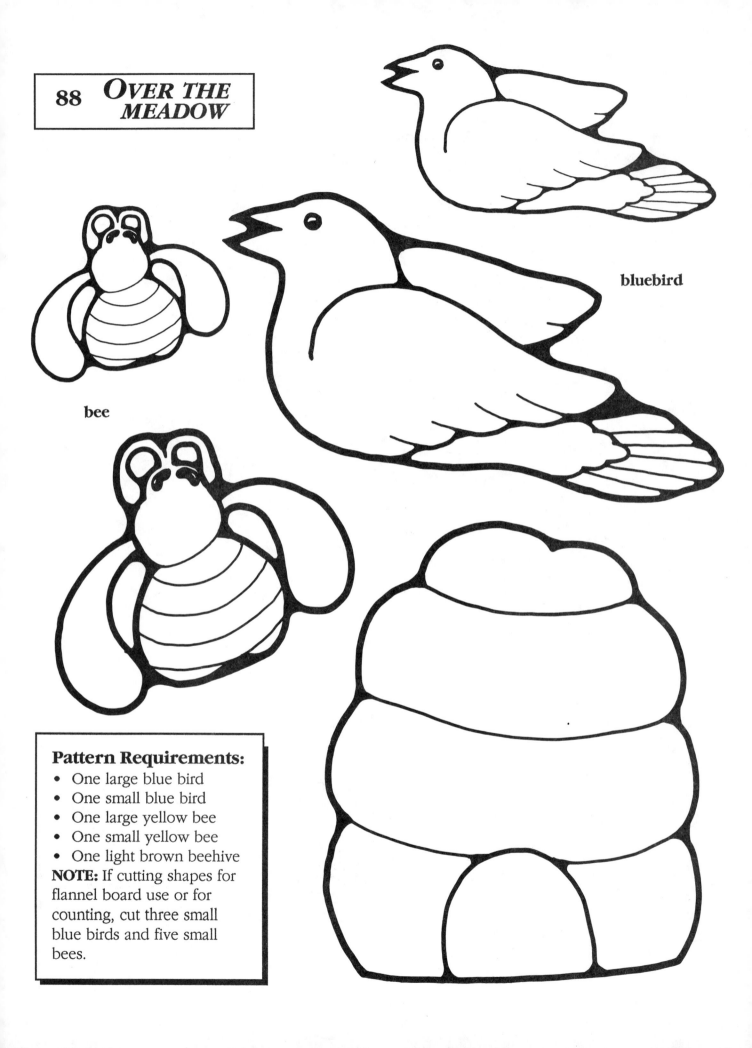

bluebird

bee

Pattern Requirements:
- One large blue bird
- One small blue bird
- One large yellow bee
- One small yellow bee
- One light brown beehive

NOTE: If cutting shapes for flannel board use or for counting, cut three small blue birds and five small bees.

sticks

crow

Pattern Requirements:
- Brown sticks; build a nest for the baby crows
- One large black crow
- One small black crow

NOTE: If cutting shapes for flannel board use or for counting, cut six small black crows.

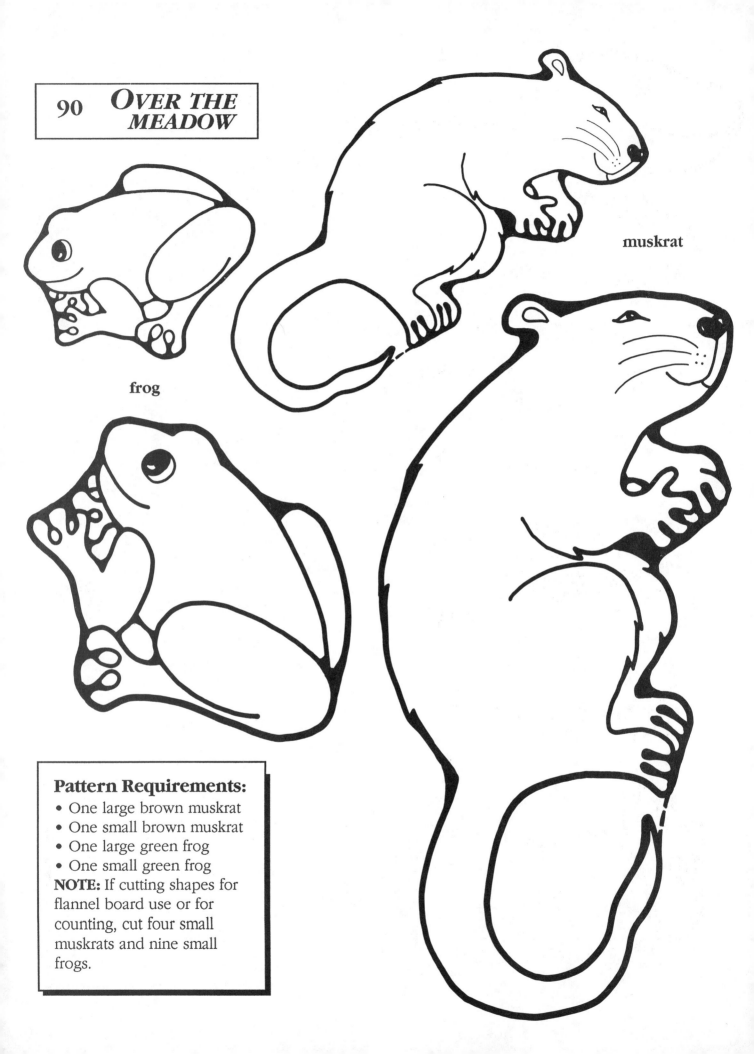

muskrat

frog

Pattern Requirements:
- One large brown muskrat
- One small brown muskrat
- One large green frog
- One small green frog

NOTE: If cutting shapes for flannel board use or for counting, cut four small muskrats and nine small frogs.

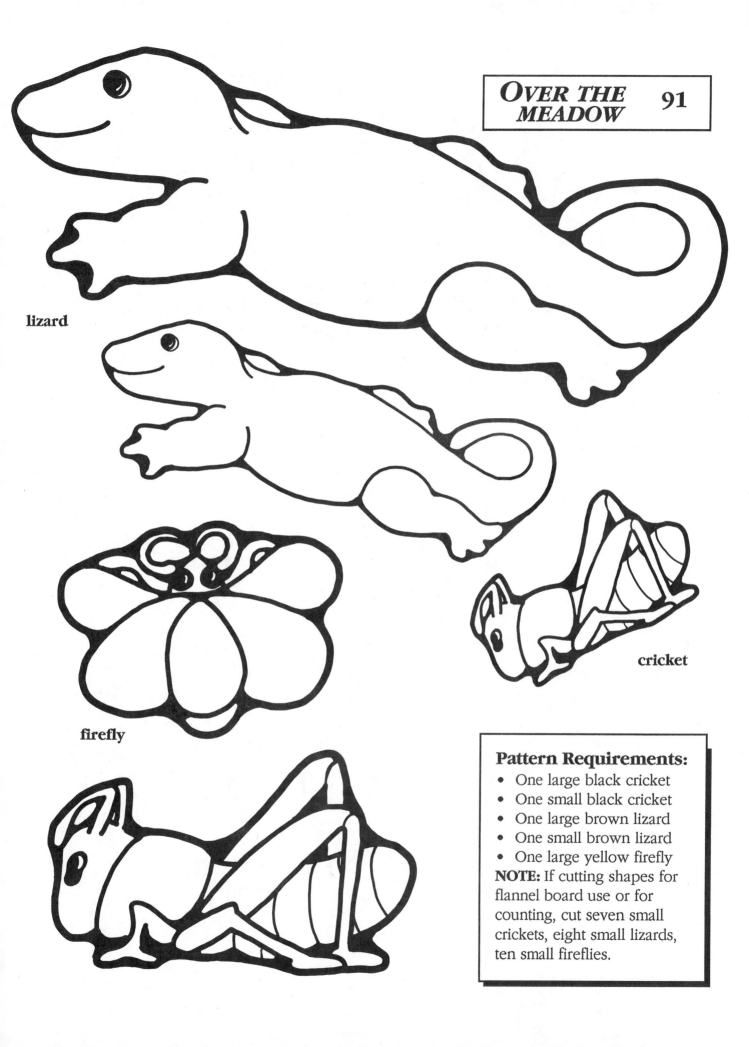

lizard

firefly

cricket

Pattern Requirements:
- One large black cricket
- One small black cricket
- One large brown lizard
- One small brown lizard
- One large yellow firefly

NOTE: If cutting shapes for flannel board use or for counting, cut seven small crickets, eight small lizards, ten small fireflies.

THE RUNAWAY BUNNY

by Margaret Wise Brown
HarperCollins

STORY SUMMARY

Once there was a little bunny who wanted to run away. With love, his mother always answers his challenges.

Helps & Hints for story integration and pattern construction found on pages 4-5.

Related Learning:
- Values
- Drawing conclusions

More To Do:
- Retell the story by creating a group mural
- Talk about time: Have you ever wanted to run away from home?

Pattern Requirements:
- One white bunny;
  add a cotton-ball tail

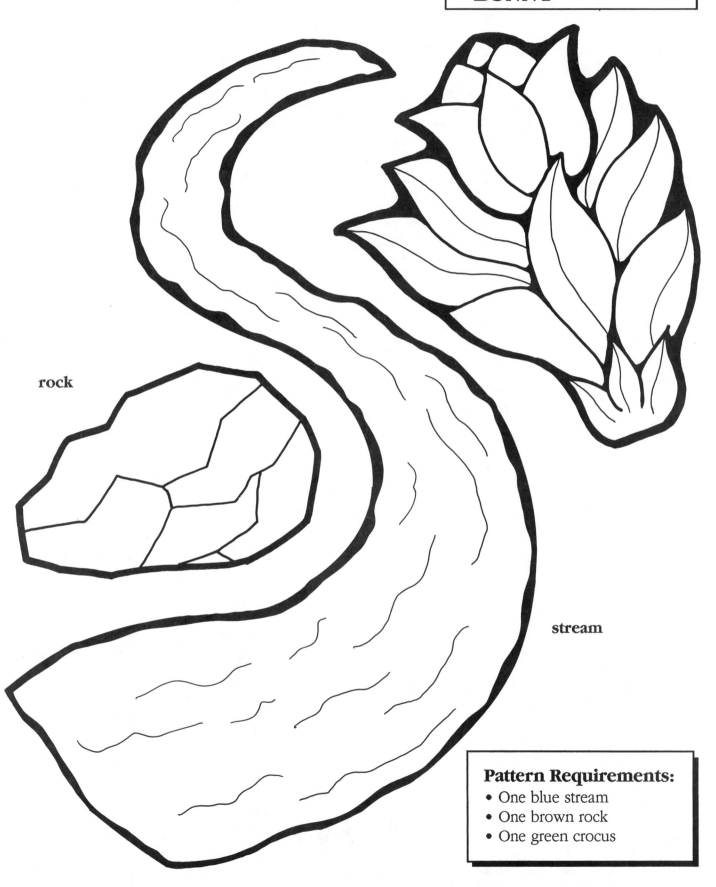

rock

stream

Pattern Requirements:
- One blue stream
- One brown rock
- One green crocus

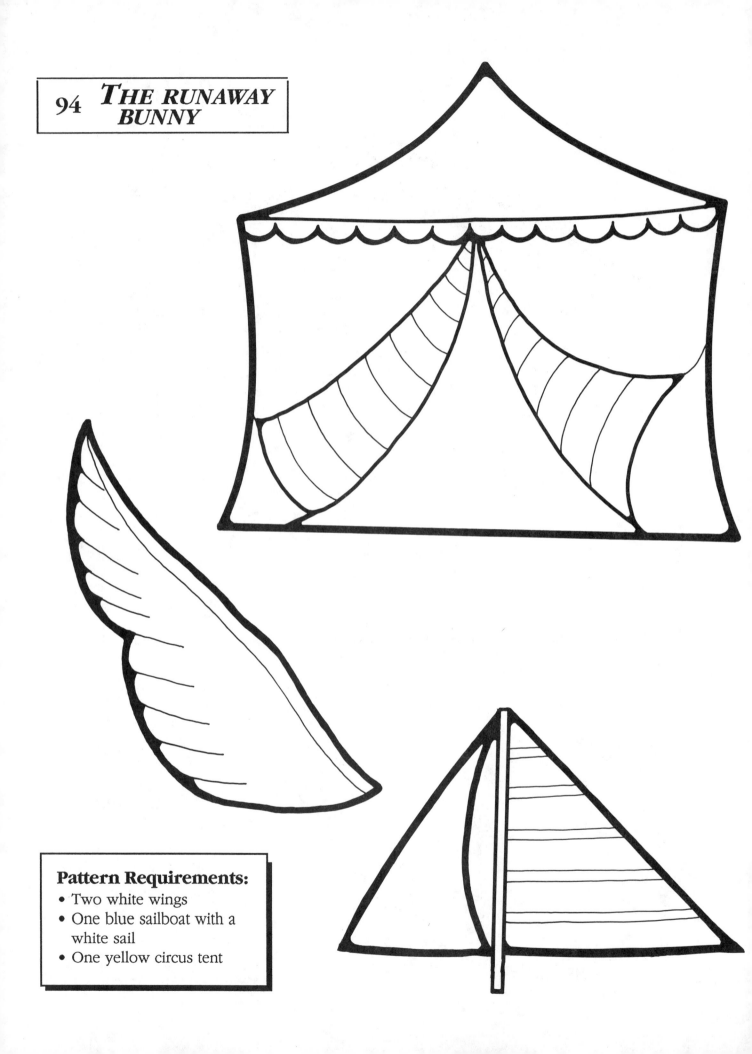

Pattern Requirements:
- Two white wings
- One blue sailboat with a white sail
- One yellow circus tent

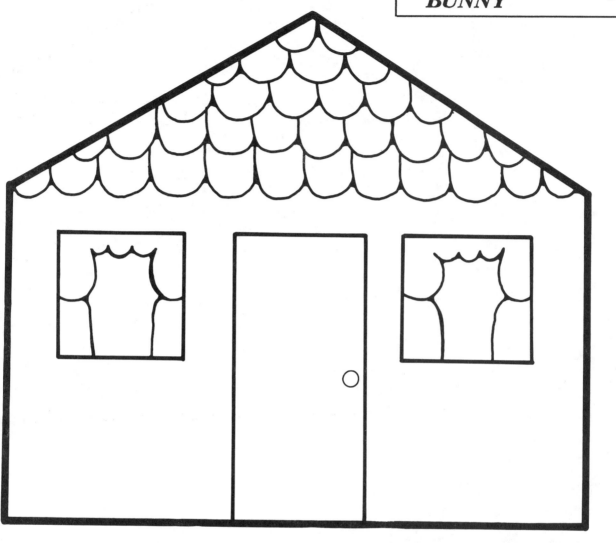

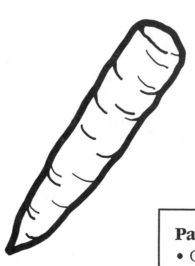

Pattern Requirements:
- One pair of blue shorts
- One orange carrot; add a green-fringed carrot top

Is Your Mama a Llama?

by Deborah Guarino
Scholastic, Inc.

Helps & Hints for story integration and pattern construction found on pages 4-5.

Story Summary

A young llama questions its animal friends about the identity of their mother, then figures out a rhyming answer.

Related Learning:
- Rhyming
- Questions, answers
- Predicting
- Identifying animals and their young

More To Do:
- Match pictures of animals and their young.
- Brainstorm a list of rhyming words.

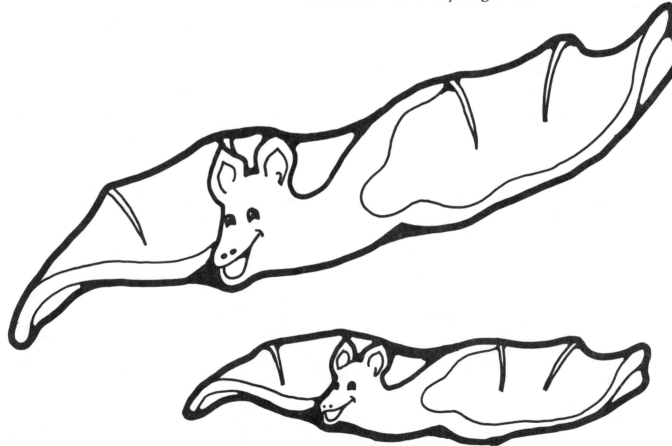

Pattern Requirements:
- One large brown bat
- One small brown bat

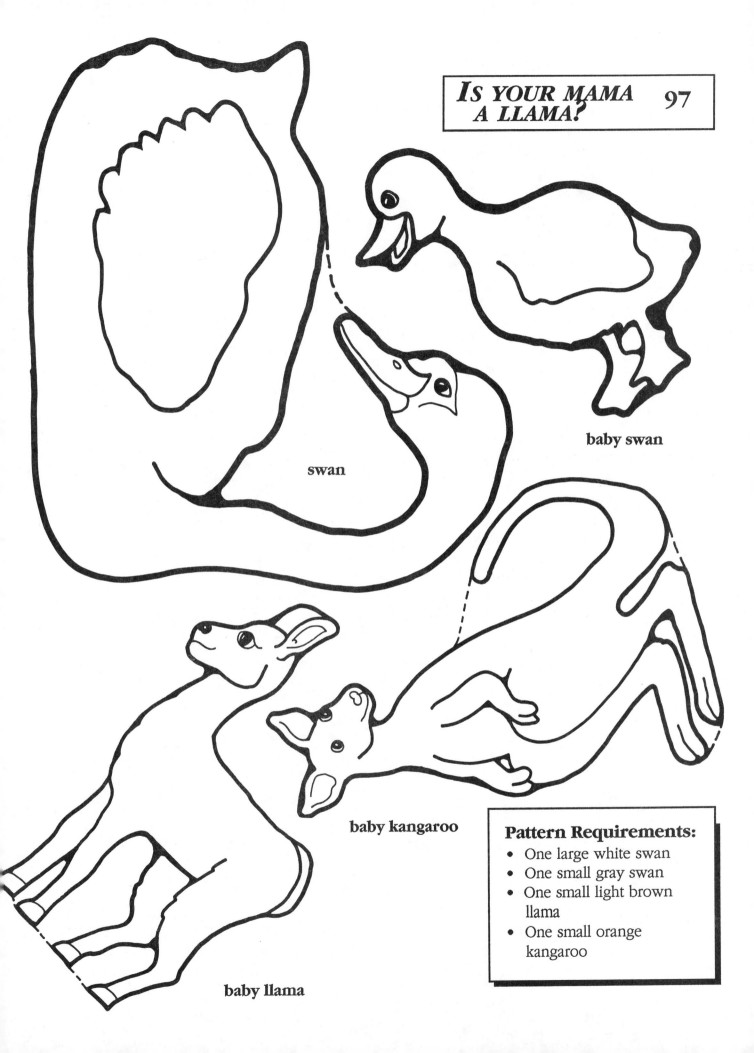

baby swan

swan

baby kangaroo

baby llama

Pattern Requirements:
- One large white swan
- One small gray swan
- One small light brown llama
- One small orange kangaroo

cow

calf

Pattern Requirements:
- One large white cow; brown spots
- One small white calf; brown spots

mama kangaroo

mama llama

Pattern Requirements:
- One large light brown llama
- One large orange kangaroo

STORY SUMMARY

A caterpillar eats its way through a great amount of food and then spins its cocoon.

THE VERY HUNGRY CATERPILLAR

by Eric Carle
The Putnam Publishing Group

Helps & Hints for story integration and pattern construction found on pages 4-5.

Related Learning:
- Counting
- Sequencing
- Life cycles

More To Do:
- Pantomime a caterpillar in a cocoon becoming a butterfly.
- Snack on—and identify—the same fruits as the caterpillar enjoyed.

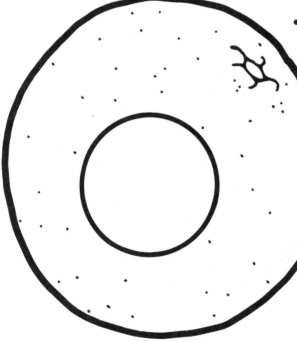

orange

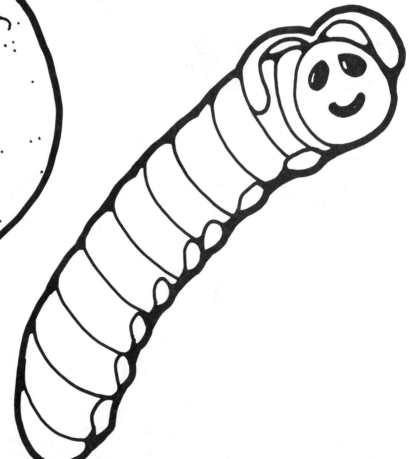

Pattern Requirements:
- One green caterpillar
- One orange orange; cut out the hole

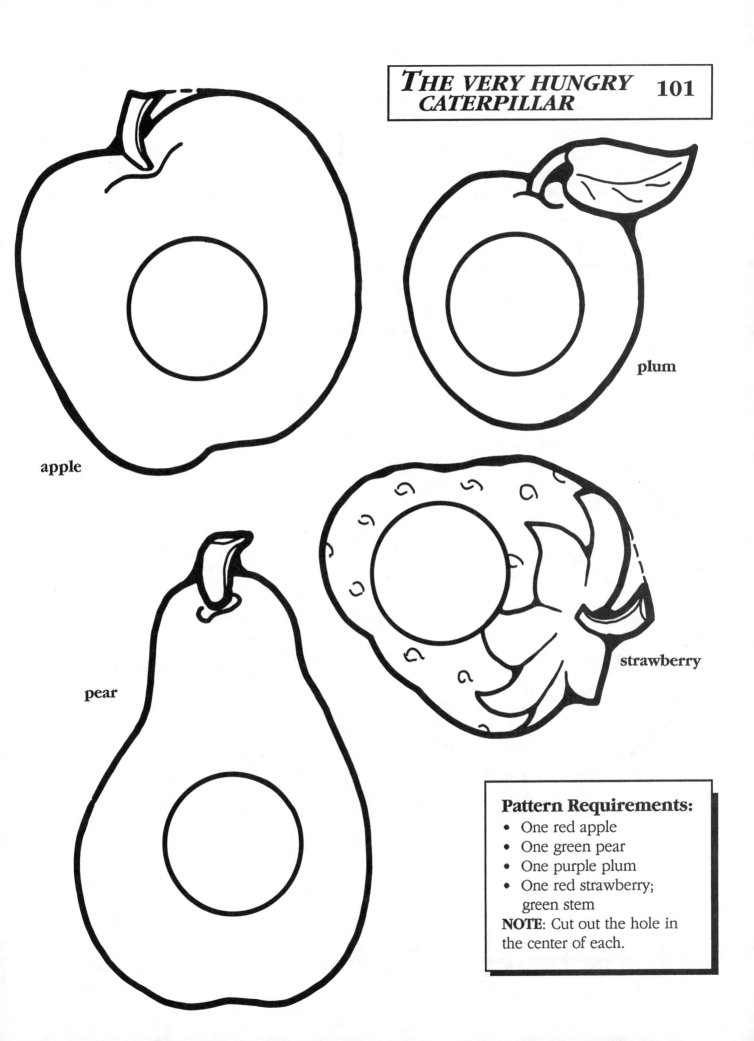

apple

plum

pear

strawberry

Pattern Requirements:

- One red apple
- One green pear
- One purple plum
- One red strawberry; green stem

NOTE: Cut out the hole in the center of each.

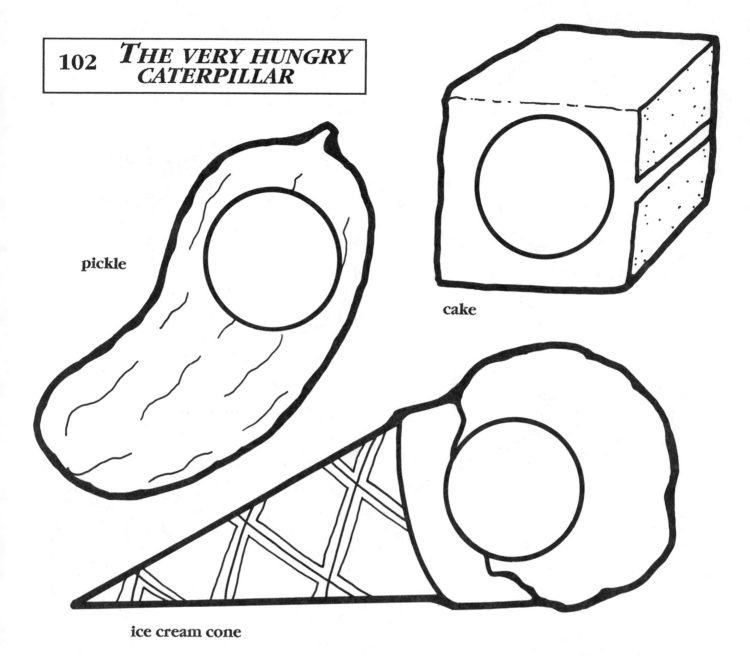

pickle

cake

ice cream cone

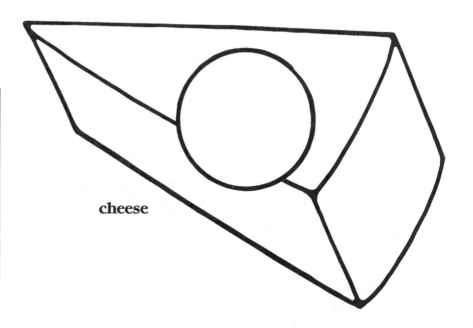

cheese

Pattern Requirements:
- One brown cake square
- One brown cone; pink ice cream
- One green pickle
- One yellow wedge of cheese

NOTE: Cut out the hole in the center of each.

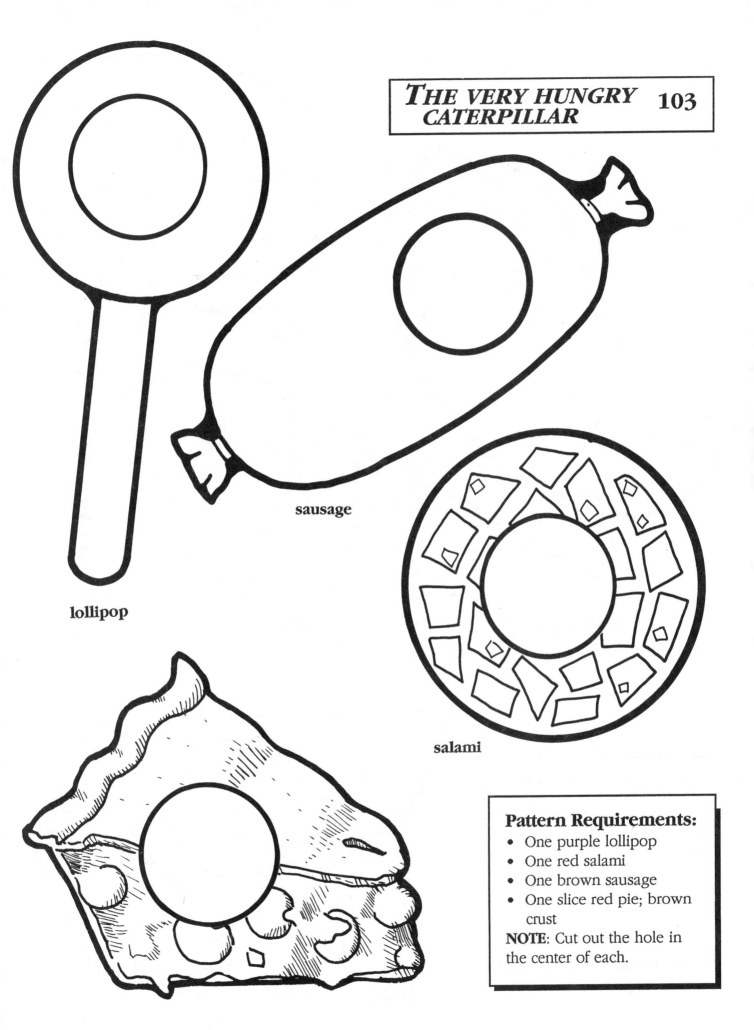

sausage

lollipop

salami

Pattern Requirements:
- One purple lollipop
- One red salami
- One brown sausage
- One slice red pie; brown crust

NOTE: Cut out the hole in the center of each.

watermelon

Pattern Requirements:

- One red watermelon slice; green rind
- One green leaf
- One white cupcake

NOTE: Cut out the hole in the center of each

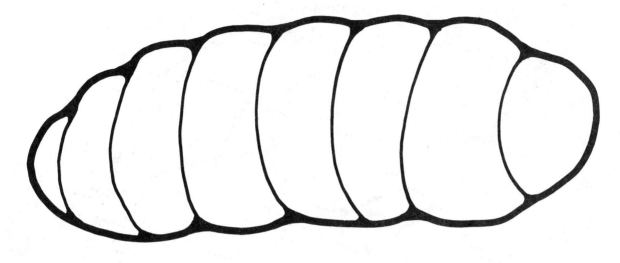

cocoon

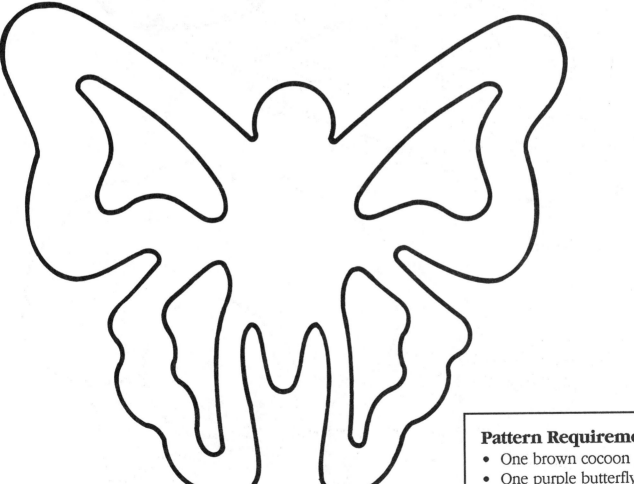

Pattern Requirements:
- One brown cocoon
- One purple butterfly; rainbow designs

PLAY WITH ME

by Marie Hall
Puffin Books

STORY SUMMARY

A young girl tries to make animal friends—with happy results and gets a lesson in patience and friendship.

Helps & Hints for story integration and pattern construction found on pages 4-5.

Related Learning:
- Directionality
- Values
- Action words

More To Do:
- Pantomime the action words in the story
- Play with a new friend for the day... or more

Pattern Requirements:
- One yellow sun
- One brown grasshopper
- One green leaf

log

pond

Pattern Requirements:
- One blue pond
- One green frog
- One brown log
- One dark brown chipmunk

Pattern Requirements:
- One green turtle
- One brown tree trunk and branches
- One white rabbit—add a cotton-ball tail

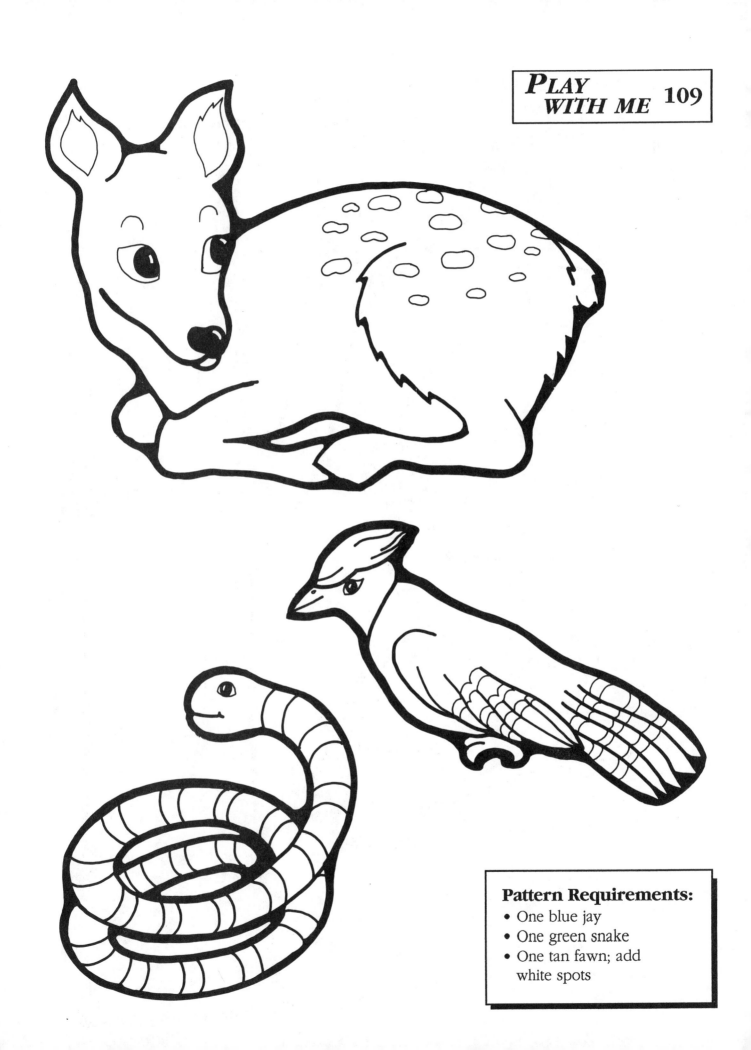

Pattern Requirements:
- One blue jay
- One green snake
- One tan fawn; add white spots

STORY SUMMARY

Sam's sister wants a sandwich. Sam has added some nasty extras! Open the flaps to find the rhyming surprises.

SAM'S SANDWICH

by David Pelham
Voyager Books

Helps & Hints for story integration and pattern construction found on pages 4-5.

Related Learning:

- Rhyming
- Following directions

More To Do:

- Plan a picnic; make sandwiches together to take along
- Follow directions and stack the ingredients in a different order

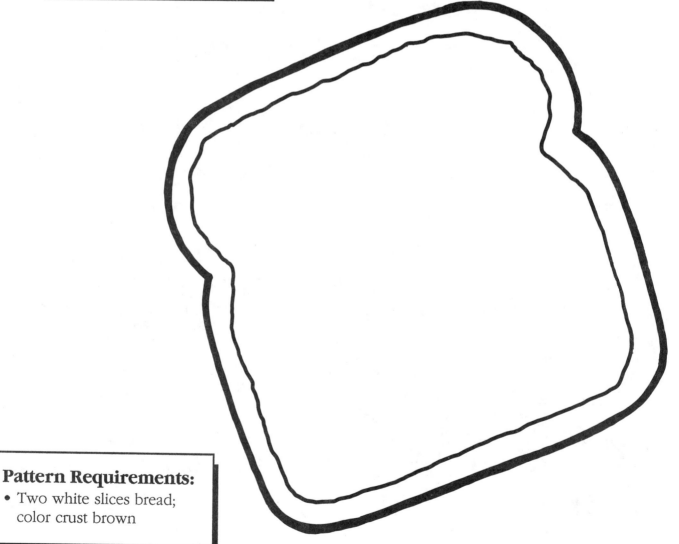

Pattern Requirements:

- Two white slices bread; color crust brown

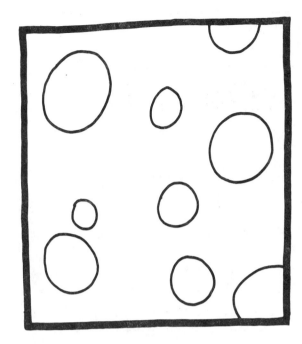

cheese

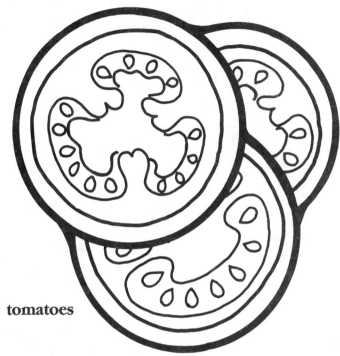

tomatoes

caterpillar

slug

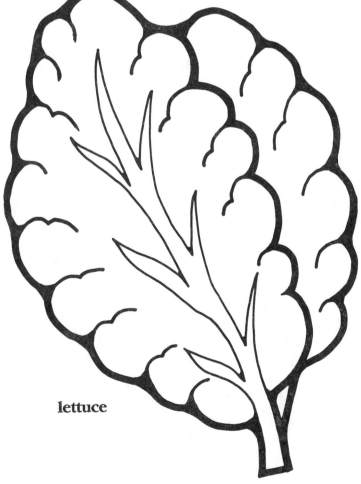

lettuce

Pattern Requirements:
- Green lettuce leaves
- One green caterpillar
- Red tomatoes
- One brown slug
- One yellow cheese slice; cut with holes

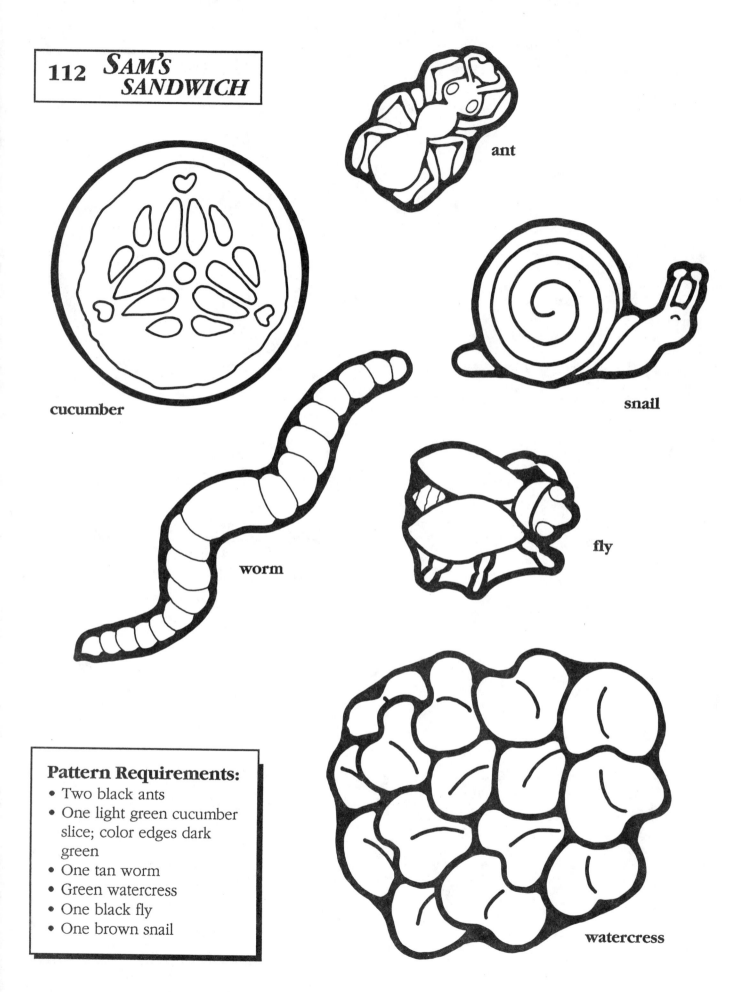

ant

cucumber

snail

worm

fly

Pattern Requirements:
- Two black ants
- One light green cucumber slice; color edges dark green
- One tan worm
- Green watercress
- One black fly
- One brown snail

watercress

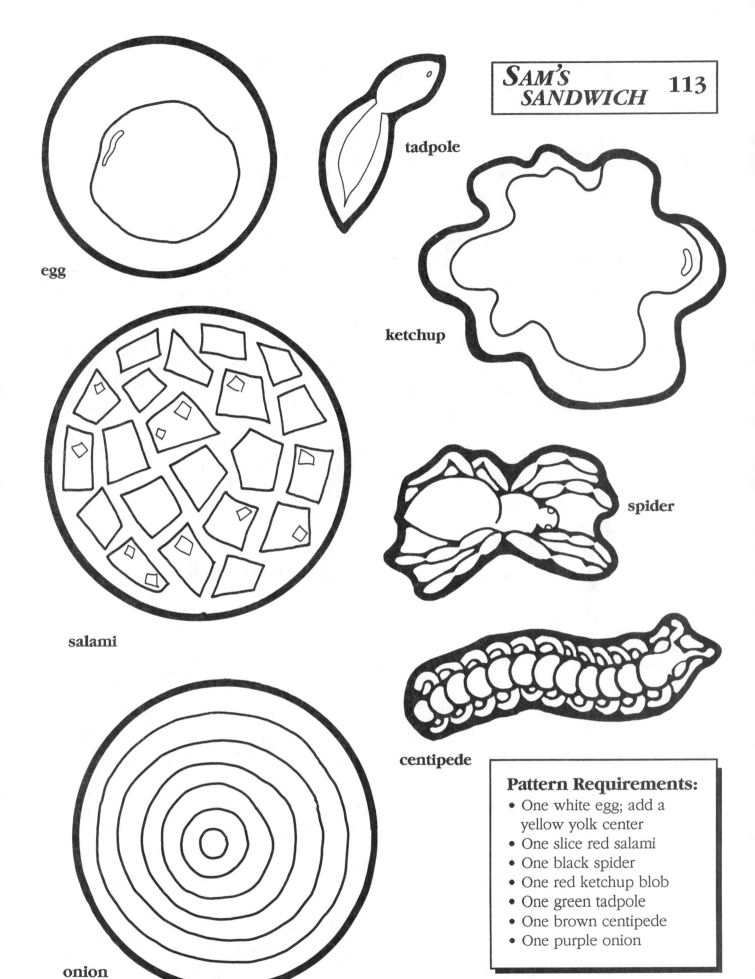

egg

tadpole

ketchup

salami

spider

centipede

onion

Pattern Requirements:
- One white egg; add a yellow yolk center
- One slice red salami
- One black spider
- One red ketchup blob
- One green tadpole
- One brown centipede
- One purple onion

If You Give a Mouse a Cookie

by Laura Numeroff
HarperCollins

STORY SUMMARY

The consequences of giving a mouse a cookie run a young host ragged.

Helps & Hints for story integration and pattern construction found on pages 4-5.

Related Learning:
- Cause and effect
- Things that are related
- Values—friendship

More To Do:
- Enjoy a snack of milk and cookies.
- Match things that "go together" such as shoes & socks.

cookie

Pattern Requirements:
- One white glass of milk
- One light brown cookie

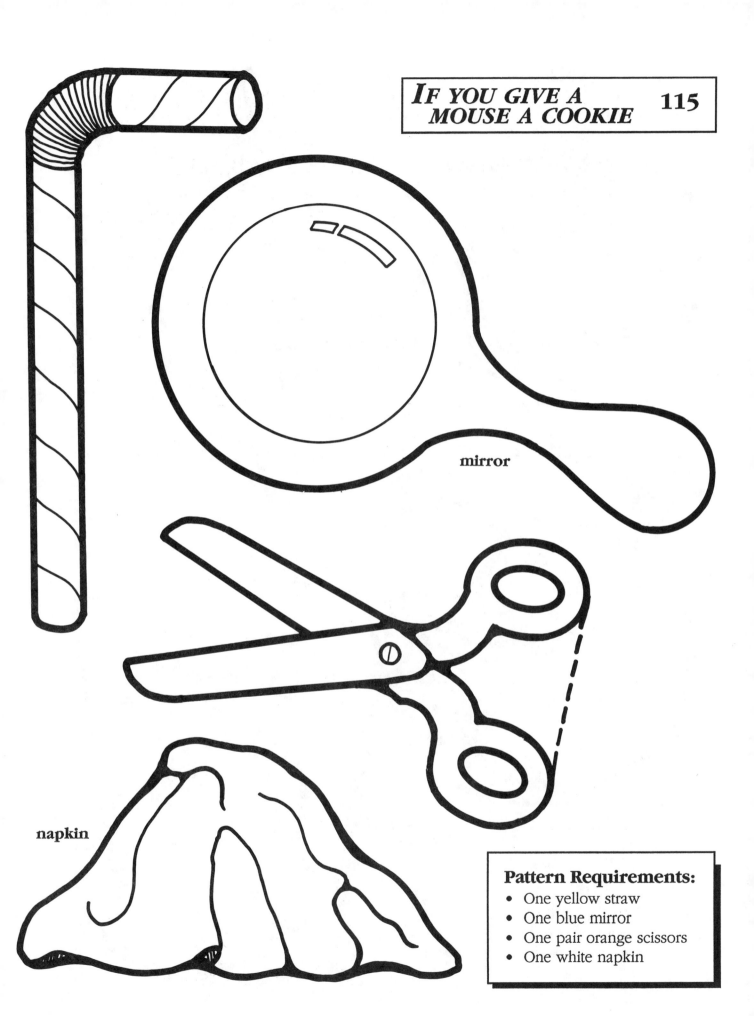

mirror

napkin

Pattern Requirements:
- One yellow straw
- One blue mirror
- One pair orange scissors
- One white napkin

mouse bed

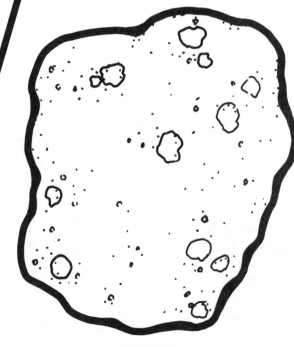

sponge

Pattern Requirements:
- One blue bucket
- One pink bed
- One yellow sponge
- One brown-handled broom; yellow bristles

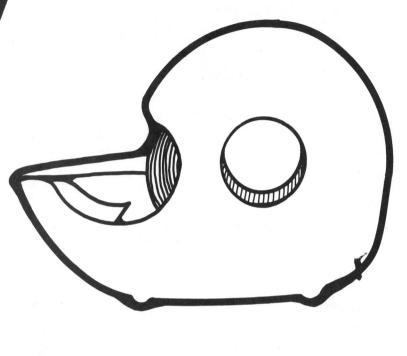

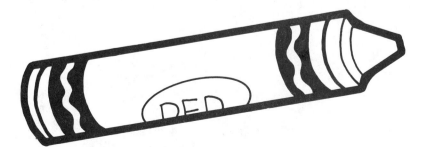

Pattern Requirements:
- One red crayon
- One orange roll of tape
- One white book
- One blue pen

CAT GOES FIDDLE-I-FEE

by Paul Galdone
Clarion Books

STORY SUMMARY

Animals share unusual sounds in repetitive, cumulative verse.

Helps & Hints for story integration and pattern construction found on pages 4-5.

Related Learning:
- Oral language
- Listening
- Repetition

More To Do:
- Make a tape recording of other silly sounds animals might make.
- Make up a movement skit to accompany the text.

hen

duck

Pattern Requirements:
- One orange hen
- One yellow duck

goose

Pattern Requirements:
- One pink pig
- One white goose
- One white sheep

Pattern Requirements:
- One light brown cow
- One dark brown horse

Pattern Requirements:
- One blue picnic basket
- One black cat
- One white dog; black spots

STORY SUMMARY

A read-along,
sing-along book that features
ocean life—
patterned after a popular
holiday carol.

12 DAYS OF SUMMER

Elizabeth Lee O'Donnell
Morrow Junior Books

Helps & Hints for story integration and pattern construction found on pages 4-5.

Related Learning:
- Counting
- Ocean animals
- Repetition
- Vocabulary development

More To Do:
- "Sing the book" as it is read aloud.
- Paint an ocean-life mural.

sea anemone

Pattern Requirements:
- One purple sea anemone
- One pink jellyfish

NOTE: If cutting shapes for flannel board use or for counting, cut three jellyfish.

jelly fish

pelican

piper

Pattern Requirements:
- One brown pelican
- One yellow piper

NOTE: If cutting shapes for flannel board use or for counting, cut two pelicans and four pipers.

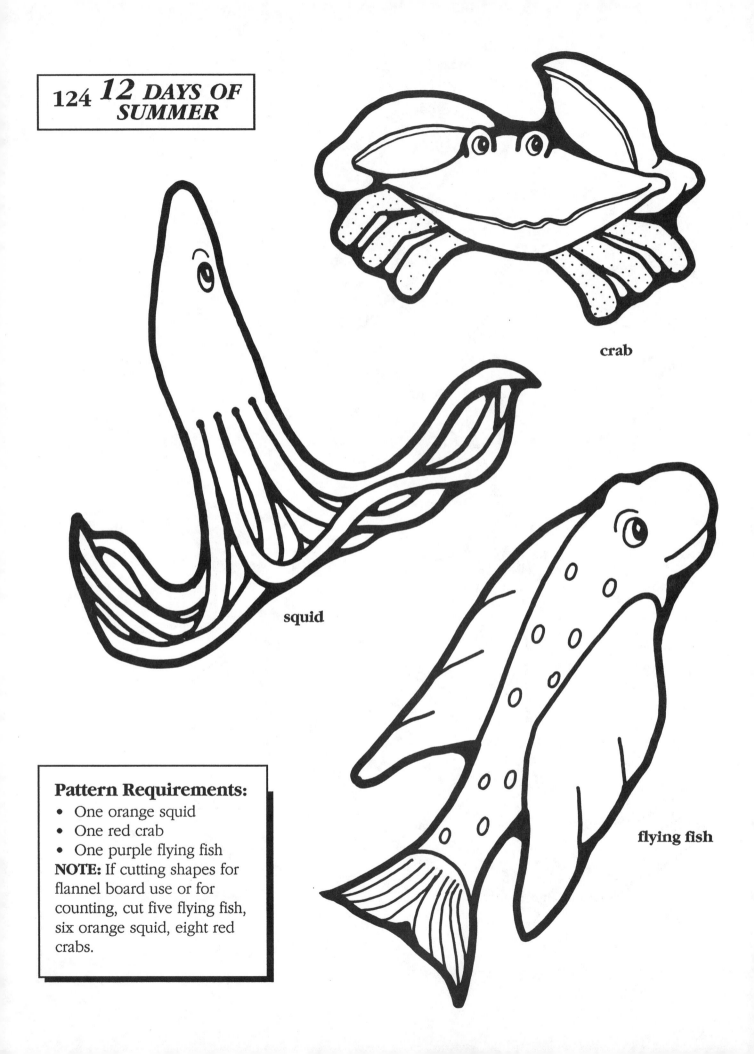

crab

squid

flying fish

Pattern Requirements:

- One orange squid
- One red crab
- One purple flying fish

NOTE: If cutting shapes for flannel board use or for counting, cut five flying fish, six orange squid, eight red crabs.

seal

Pattern Requirements:
• One gray seal
NOTE: If cutting shapes for flannel board use or for counting, cut nine seals.

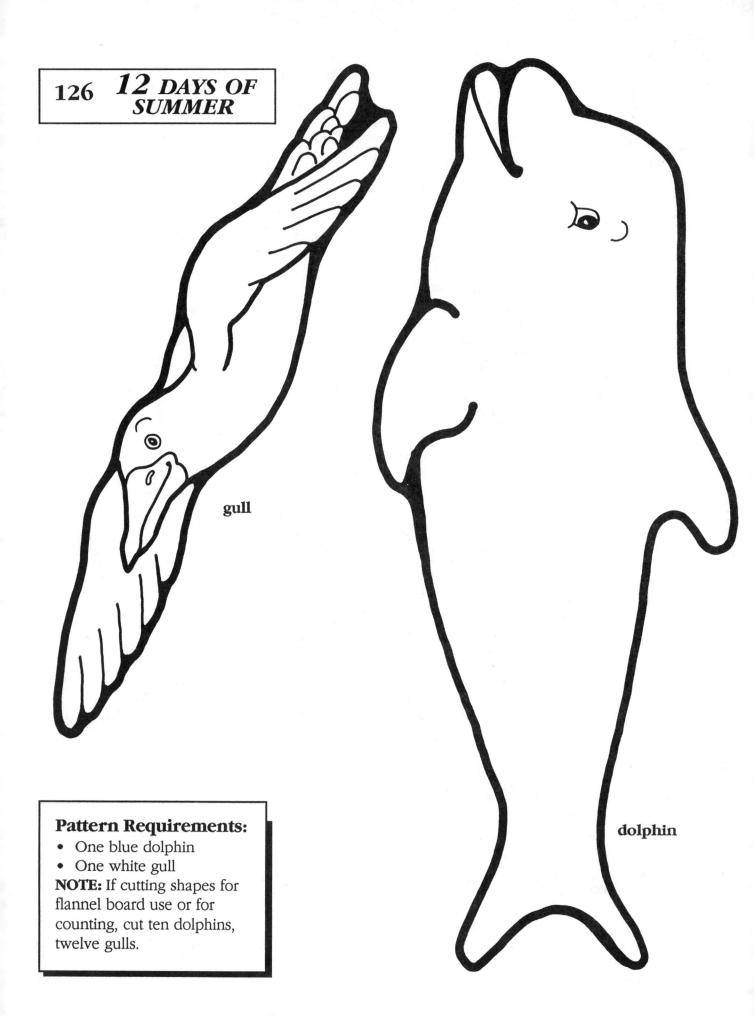

gull

dolphin

Pattern Requirements:
- One blue dolphin
- One white gull

NOTE: If cutting shapes for flannel board use or for counting, cut ten dolphins, twelve gulls.

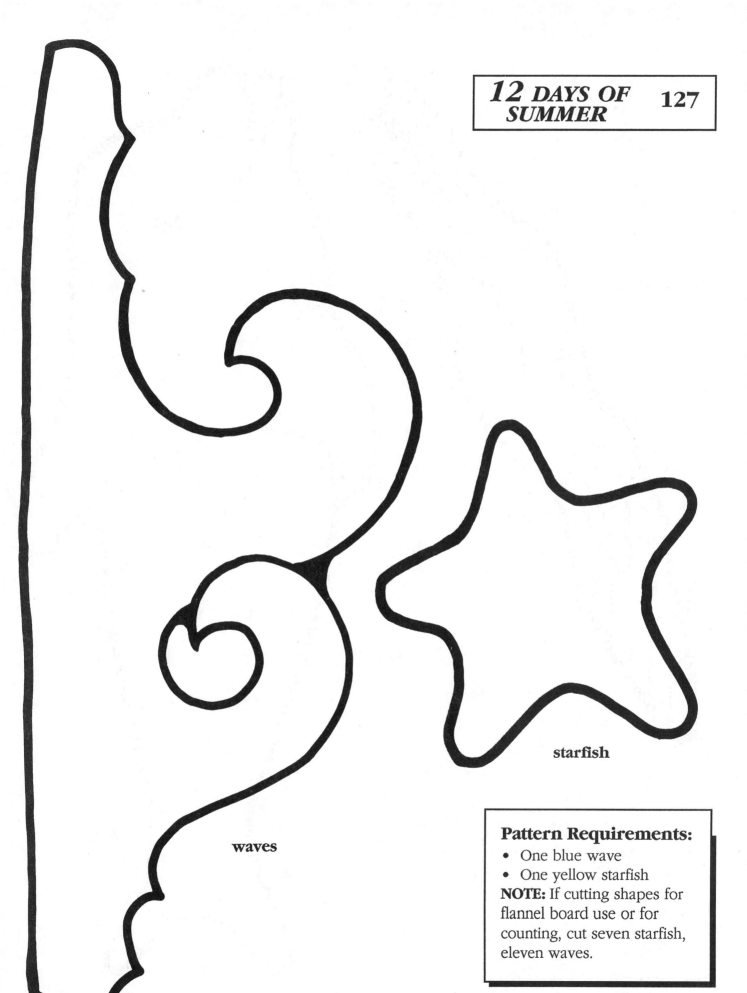

starfish

waves

Pattern Requirements:
- One blue wave
- One yellow starfish

NOTE: If cutting shapes for flannel board use or for counting, cut seven starfish, eleven waves.

More Exciting Titles from Edupress

102 Indian Activity Book
Art•Crafts•Cooking

126 Colonial Activities
Art•Crafts•Cooking

138 Frontier Activities
Art•Crafts•Cooking

148 Springboards/Starters
Multicurricular activities

139 Super Arts & Crafts
Over 700 art activites

135 Center Games
Ten easy game centers

136 Outdoor Games
Group and skill games

134 Holiday Games
Fun-filled learning

140 Classroom Kickoff
Year-long resource

123 Holiday Patterns
A host of holiday fun

124 Poem Patterns
Link poems & learning

125 Puppet Patterns
Multicurricular activities

130 Fall Projects
Multicurricular learning

131 Winter Projects
Loads of winter activities

132 Spring Projects
Apr/May/June fun

111 Lend An Ear
Build listening skills